The Beaver B...

If you're interested in animals and would like a pet of your own, here is the book for you. It helps you to choose the right kind of pet to fit in with the kind of life you and your family lead, and, having chosen, explains how to care for it properly. Dogs, cats, rabbits, mice, gerbils, hamsters, guinea pigs, birds, goldfish – even ponies – are included and there is a useful chapter on looking after wild creatures you may encounter, such as hedgehogs and injured birds. Details of feeding, housing and health care are given – in fact, everything you need to keep your pet fit and happy.

Raymond Chaplin, now a consultant for Museum and Countryside Education, is a writer and broadcaster who was formerly Education Officer for the Royal Zoological Society of Scotland and latterly Curator of the Council for Museums and Galleries in Scotland. He lives in the Scottish border country, surrounded by a varied collection of animals.

The Beaver Book of Pets

Raymond Chaplin

Illustrated by Tony Morris

Beaver Books

First published in 1979 by
The Hamlyn Publishing Group Limited
London · New York · Sydney · Toronto
Astronaut House, Feltham, Middlesex, England

© Copyright Text Raymond Chaplin 1979
© Copyright Illustrations
The Hamlyn Publishing Group Limited 1979
ISBN 0 600 37175 1

Set, printed and bound in Great Britain by
Cox & Wyman Limited, Reading
Set in Monotype Imprint

Contents

Acknowledgements

The photographs in this book were supplied by the following: Netherfield Visual Productions (© Copyright R. E. Chaplin) – Plates 1, 3, 6, 7, 8, 9, 10, 11, 12; Natural History Photographic Agency – 5; Natural History Photographic Agency (Stephen Dalton) – 2, 4; Hamlyn Publishing Group Limited – 13.

1 Choosing the right pet

For thousands of years people all over the world have set great store by the friendship and companionship to be had by sharing their life with an animal of one kind or another. Today the British and Americans are the leading pet keeping nations in the world. In Britain, with a total population of around 55 million people, for example, there are about 6 million dogs and 4.2 million cats. This means that there are few families that do not have a pet of one kind or another. Other kinds of animal are kept as pets but for obvious reasons only a small number of people keep really exotic wild animals like lions, pumas and cheetahs. This type of animal is not at all suitable as a children's pet and is more of a status symbol than anything else. Other people may keep animals not just as pets but because they wish to observe and study them and are fascinated by their behaviour and needs. Several friends of mine keep snakes and lizards and as well as being fond of them and interested in them they also like to study them. Pond life has always fascinated me and most years I like to set up an aquarium of pond life to watch it develop through spring into summer. You wouldn't really call the water boatmen and tadpoles pets as such but I shall include them in this book because it is all about you and me keeping animals in captivity and all that that involves.

When you take an animal and keep it in captivity you become totally responsible for it just as your mother and father are responsible for you. Think carefully about what that means. That very attractive little puppy or kitten, for example, is going to come into your family just like you did when you were a baby. In the wild it would have been brought up by its parents, fed, cleaned and protected by them. They would teach it how to look after itself, to catch its own food and to cope with all the dangers and threats of the world. Now instead, it is you and your family that are going to carry out all these tasks and more for quite a few years. In the beginning the pet won't be house trained – that, by the way, is just a polite way of saying that when it wants to go to the toilet it will go there and then. Until you teach it to go regularly out of doors the house is going to be full of little accidents to be cleaned up. It will also be sick from time to time. Your life won't be your own either. Play and lots of it is a natural part of growing up and learning about life for all young mammals, normally carried out in a family group with its brothers and sisters. You now take their place and it is you who will have to roll and romp and chase with your puppy which actually is great fun and jolly good exercise and should make you and your pet firm friends. At the same age, though, it is also going to chew things it shouldn't and generally make mischief. Don't be surprised if your favourite teddy bear gets chewed up! Once the first few months are over it is a very different matter and if you have looked after it properly you will have a fit, healthy and well behaved companion which will be part of your family for many years.

I have written about a dog which is a good example of a pet that is very demanding on everyone but which also makes a great contribution to family life. This or a cat is the sort of animal that we are often thinking of when we are seeking a pet. Others such as hamsters and budgerigars are not so demanding in their needs and for this reason we should take a very good look at just what is involved in keeping different kinds of pet and what we can expect from them. In this way we can make a choice of a suitable children's pet that will have every chance of being a successful one.

You shouldn't just take your birthday money or whatever and go into a pet shop and bring home what you fancy. Think of the animal and of your family. Before you get your pet you must have all the things that it will need and you will also want to have your parents' and maybe brothers' and sisters' support. They might at first not be very keen on the idea of a pet and you will see why in a minute. But if you have carefully worked out what is involved you have a good chance of being able to persuade them that you really will look after it. So let us have a look at what you have got to take into account.

What kind of pets are you allowed to keep in your house or flat?

You probably haven't thought about that, but in quite a few places there are rules about what you may keep. In many blocks of flats, for example, local councils may have a complete ban on pets. Often they have in mind dogs and cats and wouldn't really object to a tank of fish or a hamster but you certainly couldn't keep pigeons. Most privately owned houses do not restrict you from keeping ordinary pets but you may not be able to keep pigs or ponies. Talk things over with your family first and get your parents to check any rules and regulations that may apply to pet keeping.

How much space would your pet need?

A dog, for example, does not need very much room to sleep and lie around in. He will readily share a part of your house. However, if you have only a little space indoors be careful of the size of dog you choose because he will take up quite a lot of that space and can be very clumsy. My own Labrador has a very strong tail and often knocks over the cups and saucers from the coffee table as he welcomes someone home. Another is fond of going to sleep with its head under the coffee table and you have to be careful how you wake him up otherwise the whole lot goes over. The space that a dog really needs, though, is for exercise, and they do need plenty of this. Most dogs need several miles of walking and running each day to keep them fit, healthy and happy. If you have not got any open spaces near by this exercise will have to be given by you on foot with a lead twice a day whatever the weather. A near by open space will enable your dog to get in plenty of exercise without much effort from you, especially if friends have a

9

dog and you can exercise them together. This also makes for a more natural social life for your dog which still retains most of the traits, habits and needs of its wild ancestors which are rather different from those of human beings. Always go out with your dog and never leave him to exercise himself alone.

Most owners leave their cats to take their own exercise especially at night and may have little idea of what happens whilst they are asleep. Although cats are active by day their natural instinct is to be out and about at night; their eyesight, for example, is adapted for this. You may find that some individuals are less inclined to be out at night than others. In most cats you will not destroy this instinct by changing their routine and shutting them in at night. This will save your pet from coming home having been in a fight with other cats or injured by dogs, foxes or even owls, and, especially by motor vehicles. Many cats are killed on the road not only at night but during the day as well and if you live near a busy road, and your cat roams free, there is every likelihood that your pet will be killed or injured. If you do live amongst busy roads you should consider most carefully whether you could or should have a cat or not.

Birds such as budgerigars and canaries which are gregarious social birds by nature often spend much of their lives alone shut up in small cages, something of which I strongly disapprove, yet they are sold in their tens of thousands every year. They are not quite as unhappy if this is their home base from which at some time during the day they have the freedom of flying round the room and generally exercising. There is, however, no comparison to my mind between birds kept indoors like that and a group that live free in an outdoor aviary with a roomy flight cage. In general most animals have a comparatively small space which they regard as their home – for humans it is a house, for a bird or hamster a cage – here they will normally eat and sleep and have protection and shelter. In addition to that they will want to use a bigger area to satisfy many other instinctive behavioural needs, and in satisfying these they will also take their exercise. In a wild animal living free we would call this latter area the animal's home range, by which we mean the area over which he will normally range to find food, search for a mate and so on; it is his living space.

Would a pet fit in with the family timetable?
Although a lot of animals readily adjust to a family routine there are limits beyond which their natural instincts and needs should not be pushed. Dogs, cats, horses and ponies (especially if stabled) need attention during the day. If they do not get this horses and ponies can become seriously ill or may injure themselves. Dogs and cats may be able to cope with being shut in during a short working day, say 8.30 a.m. – 4 p.m., but not with a longer one, perhaps from 7 a.m. – 6 p.m. Dogs in particular, once they have been toilet trained, are very unwilling to relieve themselves in the house and are extremely upset if they have to do so. Cats can be provided with an indoor toilet tray and also with a hinged flap in an external door so that they can come and go as they wish. For an adult cat a prolonged absence through the day is less of a hardship than for a dog. For dogs, horses and ponies and young animals including kittens, a long absence during the day would be positively cruel. You should not, therefore, consider keeping these animals if someone is not on hand to look after them and to keep an eye on them for most of the time.

What will happen to your pet when you go on holiday?
Are there friends or neighbours who will look after it or can you take it on holiday with you? Remember that if you are going abroad on holiday you cannot take your pet with you. Some pets, such as fish, can with special arrangements be left for greater or lesser periods but you can't do this with dogs or cats.

It is generally possible to have your dog or cat boarded at kennels while you are away. Demand for boarding places is heavy, and you should book well in advance. There are, unfortunately, few places that will look after other pets, although in a few areas there are from time to time people offering this service either in your home or on their own premises. Inevitably boarding or pet care services are quite costly and it may be worth coming to a reciprocal arrangement with friends or neighbours to look after pets, indoor plants, and so on. If you do this, however, do be especially careful of two things. Firstly, that they have pets of their own and do know and care about looking after them properly. Secondly, it always seems to me that the minute the owner goes away a previously healthy animal gets sick or injured, or it runs away or something equally disastrous happens. If you leave your pet in someone's care always plan for the worst and leave clear instructions as to what should be done in the event of sickness or injury, along with discretionary powers to act in conjunction with the vet in the case of serious injury. How much are you prepared to pay for an operation following an accident, and how much care and attention can and are you prepared to give to your pet in recovering from an accident? You probably hadn't thought about this at all and it would be a very difficult decision for your friend to make. Be fair, be realistic; if you must go away and leave your pets they are still your responsibility even if someone else is coping with the problems.

Different animals live for different lengths of time. Most dogs, for example, will easily live to ten or more years whilst the larger parrots will make thirty years or more, and many reptiles properly looked after are also long lived. Small mammals like hamsters and mice have a much shorter life span, rarely more than a year or two. Think about how long your pet might live. The table on page 13 will help you. Many of the animals bought as pets are quite unsuitable for the people who have bought them and often they do not know how or don't have the facilities to care for them properly. They are not being deliberately cruel, but the animal is not happy and rarely flourishes. A good example of this is a tortoise. Very few people can look after a tortoise properly in this country; they are a frustrating and unrewarding pet for the average family and something like 98 per cent of them bought in the early summer die before the year is out. (There is another good reason for not keeping a tortoise as a pet, which you will see on page 131.) Another reason for the early death of pets is that there is very little expert supervision of the pet trade, and there is a fringe of dealers whose stock is not in the best of health or condition. Most of the blame however, is to be put on the owners of the pets through a lack of knowledge of the animals' needs. Bad pet stores are very easily recognised and they should not be patronised.

Likely lifespan of selected pets

These figures are only a very rough guide to the likely length of life of these animals in captivity as pets when properly cared for and excluding the effects of serious illness or accident.

Dog	10–15 years
Cat	12–18 years
Rabbit	5–7 years
Guinea pig	3–6 years
Mouse	1–2 years
Hamster	1–2 years
Gerbil	2–3 years
Budgerigar	5–7 years
Parrot	20–30 years
Tortoise	10–20 years
Pony	18–25 years

Can you afford your pet?

I don't just mean to buy it but to actually accommodate and feed it. Keeping a dog, for example, can be quite expensive, and in addition to the everyday running costs there are veterinary bills for regular vaccinations as well as for treatments. The table below will give you some idea of the costs of keeping each animal, with the cost of buying it, accommodating it and a regular feeding bill. There is also an estimate of veterinary costs. These figures were worked out in June 1978, so don't forget to correct them for current prices. The following table will give you a very rough idea of what it will cost to buy and keep your pet. In some cases you will be able to obtain your pet for less than the figure given. The price given is the approximate price of these animals from a reputable breeder. The actual price will depend on the breed or variety chosen and in some cases whether the animal is of show standard or not, in which case you could pay considerably more. In the text I have suggested ways in which the costs of keeping your pet can be reduced so that you should be able to cut some of these costs.

Guide to costs

Price	Weekly cost of food	Medication and treatment	Additional costs
large dog £45–£90	£5	£25	few
Small dog (e.g. Spaniel) £25–£50	£2.25	£25	few
Cat £10–£40	£1.50	£15	few
Rabbit £5–£30	winter £1 summer 25p	rarely needed	hutch and run £8–£15
Guinea pig £5–£10	winter 75p summer 25p	rarely needed	hutch and run £8–£15
Mouse £1.50–£10	30p	rarely needed	cage £6
Hamster £2–£5	25p	rarely needed	cage £6
Gerbil £2–£3	30p	rarely needed	cage £6
Budgerigar £5–£10	40p	rarely needed	cage £10–£20
Parrot from £75	£1	rarely needed	cage and perches £40
Tortoise £3–£5	50p	rarely needed	few
Pony 11.2 h.h. £150	*	£50	Considerable; tack, clothing, transport insurance, shoeing, grazing, stabling etc.
Horse 15 h.h. £500	*	£60	

*Feeding costs of horses and ponies vary tremendously according to how the animal is kept and worked and where and when food is purchased. More detailed advice is essential if considering keeping a horse – see text and further reading list.

What should you keep as a pet?

In Britain many years ago, (as in some European countries today) the keeping of wild song-birds was very popular and large numbers such as linnets and nightingales were trapped and sold in the markets. Today it is illegal to keep most British wild birds and to take any species from the wild. It is not illegal, however, to keep wild species if the bird was bred in captivity and is close-ringed to verify this. It is, in some circumstances, possible to get a licence to keep certain wild birds. Only a few of our wild mammals, reptiles and amphibians have the same kind of protection and in most cases it would not be illegal to keep one, although they do not in general make good pets for the average family. The reason for this prohibition on the keeping of wild birds is very much tied up with their preservation and conservation in the wild and we need to be very aware of the threats to the world's wildlife posed by the pet trade. It will raise in your mind the question of whether or not you want to keep a foreign pet in view of what goes on. There is a huge multi-million pound international trade in wild animals, most of it between the poorer countries and the richer ones. Millions of animals, especially birds, are involved in this trade and for every one that reaches the pet market a great many more die on the way. Although there is some attempt at control it is largely ineffectual and despite attempts to provide better travel conditions for these animals thousands die and suffer in transit. A lot of wildlife is being taken and a great deal of suffering is being caused to supply animals to the pet trade for you and me. Britain now controls the importation of wild animals into this country which has put a great premium on breeding from animals in captivity, a step that must be welcomed by all. In the past few people bothered to try and breed them as it was easier and cheaper to import new stock from the wild. For example, hamsters and gerbils, budgerigars, dogs, cats and guinea pigs as well as many fish are all bred in captivity for the pet trade so that they are not subject to the same stresses as animals caught in the wild. It is regrettable, though, that each year large numbers of tortoises are taken from the wild in southern Europe and imported under appalling conditions for the pet trade. They are all taken from the wild and no attempt is made to breed them in captivity. I do not believe that tortoises make good pets for the majority of families and the vast numbers that die each year would support this conclusion.

Where should you get your pet from?

There are a number of possible sources and each is worth exploring. Pet rabbits, guinea pigs, mice and gerbils are often bred very successfully by children and there may well be someone in your street or class at school who has some surplus which they have bred. As long as the animals look healthy and have a good temperament they are a source to be encouraged. The same is true of many of the smaller birds. A great many people breed cage birds such as budgerigars and canaries as well as other species and it is very likely that there is a local breeder near to you. Look out for adverts in your local paper or at your local shop's 'For Sale' board. Be very careful about the purchase of puppies and kittens from local sources to discourage irresponsible breeding. Unfortunately, some cat and dog owners allow their female dogs and cats to become pregnant by any roving male and to regularly produce litters which they either give away, turn loose or even drown. I do not feel that one should encourage these people in any way. I am also against buying, in the majority of cases, puppies and kittens from High Street pet shops where these are not carefully bred pedigree animals. Charming as many mongrels are they are all too often the result of irresponsible breeding, and may not have been properly cared for when young. It is this kind of thing that one wishes to prevent. By purchasing from either a professional or private breeder you are sure of obtaining an animal of good quality and health that has been carefully bred for a purpose and which will have the characteristics of the breed or cross selected.

Temperament is a very important factor in the choice of an individual animal and also in the type of breed which you choose. One tends to think of temperament mostly in relation to dogs, but it is a factor in all kinds of animal from hamsters to rabbits and cats. By going directly you have the opportunity of comparing the produce of different breeders, of choosing a particular individual and of having an assurance of temperament and other qualities.

There is a further possible source of a pet and that is from a cat or dog home where stray animals are taken. These can only be kept for a very short time and if they are not claimed or homes are not found for them they have to be put down. I would urge you, if you can, to try one of these places for a suitable animal. All kinds end up there, including young puppies and kittens of the best breeds, which clearly cost a lot of money but which the owners became fed up with and just turned loose. The period just after Christmas is especially bad but the same thing goes on all year round. Another bad time is the summer holiday period when pets are just turned loose whilst the family goes away. It is almost unbelievable isn't it, but it goes on all the time. If you go to a home for stray animals the manager will be able to give you a lot of help and advice about your choice and will make very certain that the right match is being made before he lets you have one.

The best place to purchase fish is from a local specialist dealer. Most large towns have at least one such shop where a wide selection of species is kept and expert help and advice are available. Such shops are usually in close touch with local aquarist societies whose members can be of great help to the young enthusiast.

In a large town you may well find a pet store that stocks a range of birds and mammals, and by looking at the conditions in which they are kept you will be able to judge whether or not the shop is a good source of stock or not. There are a number of professional bodies for the pet trade and most of the better stores will belong to one of these.

On a national basis, the weekly newspaper *Cage and Aviary Bird* has features on keeping and breeding many animals besides birds, and their advertisement columns are the principal means of advertisement for sale of all kinds of livestock available from private breeders, fanciers and the specialist traders. If you are interested in a particular kind of pet or even a particular breed, it is certain that there will be either a national society with local branches or a local society devoted to it. The secretary will be pleased to hear of your interest and will be able to put you in touch with breeders and members who have stock available. Names and addresses of local societies may be found in the specialist journals, or your local library will probably be able to help you.

It will pay you from the outset to get only the best healthy stock from a reputable source and this should go a long way to ensuring a happy and healthy association between you and your chosen pet.

2 How to keep your pet

If you are going to be a really successful pet keeper you will need to study the requirements of your pet and to devise ways of providing them. The needs of most of the animals we regularly keep as pets are generally well known but every individual is different, and by watching carefully and taking note you will discover what is right for your own pet. Exactly the same approach is used in zoological collections where often the species are little known. Success then depends on the knowledge and experience of the staff with similar species and the sympathetic care and determination of the keeper on the spot. First of all read all you can about other people's experiences of keeping your kind of pet and also other related animals – you never know when the information might be useful and you will learn a lot of new ideas. Also find out how your pet would live in the wild so that you can gain an insight into how it should be looked after in captivity. Try to keep notes on the books you read and on what other experts have told you and also keep records about how you look after your pet and how it behaves.

The importance of understanding the needs of your pet, whatever they are, can best be illustrated by taking some examples of animals regularly kept as pets and considering in detail what their natural way of life would be in the wild. We can then consider how these needs can be met now when they are kept as pets.

The ancestors of your pet evolved a means of living and breeding in their natural wild habitat. The way they behave, what they eat, when they are active, how they breed, how they get on with each other and with other species are a part of the way of life that evolved to ensure the survival of the species. In almost all animals kept as pets these basic instincts still influence the way in which the animal lives even if it and its parents have never known the wild state. Each individual may also to some extent have had its natural behaviour patterns modified by contact with human beings in that it may have been taught not to do something that was part of its instincts to do. In other cases certain characteristics may have been bred out of a species or a particular characteristic carefully bred for. In dogs, for example, Labradors are bred with an excellent safe temperament, but the large size of the original working strain is no longer encouraged. Foxhounds are rigorously selected for hunting and retrievers for recovering shot birds. The relationship between man and dog is only possible because of the basic social make up of the wolf which is the wild ancestor of most, if not all, of our domestic dogs.

It follows that if we are to keep an animal as a pet so that it will be really happy and contented, we must organise things so that these basic instincts are taken care of. This is the art of good husbandry for all kinds of animal. Some examples will illustrate how, in general terms, we can reconcile these basic instincts of the species in the domestic situation.

Your dog, if he were running wild, would be a member of a pack in which he would spend most of his life. Within that pack he would know his place and his relationship with each individual. The pack would have a leader and there would be a hierarchy of who bossed whom, although this would not be asserted all the time. You can think of it in much the same way as a large family and how everyone relates to each other in it. This pack would have a hunting territory or area which would be large enough to supply its needs. Within that range strangers would rarely be tolerated. Because of the need to move around there would not be fixed sleeping areas although secure safe places would be known and used whenever possible. Life in the pack depends very much on its members so that their welfare and that of the young is a basic factor.

*In the wild your dog would be part of a pack
- a large family*

Because they are hunters they must be fit and active, and being carnivores, we must think of them as getting most of their food needs from meat (flesh), bones and the plants and other food in the gut of their prey. This latter is a particularly important source of semi-digested plant food which most carnivores seem to need to keep them in tip-top condition. Carnivores eat to the full when there is food and are then largely inactive until they are hungry again.

In feeding an adult dog you can follow this pattern by giving him one meal a day, generally in the evening. When full after his meal he will prefer to sleep. So you must arrange to fit his hunting (i.e. exercise) in during the day, which is also the time when he will enjoy lazing around gnawing at a bone. When you feed your dog properly you will also be following the wild pattern of providing the total prey. Meat itself, fed alone would result in a malnourished, unfit individual. A balanced feed is obtained by feeding a mixture of a good biscuit meal with meat according to the manufacturer's instructions or by feeding a commercial complete food. These, however, look more like a porridge, and though they are excellent there is one thing lacking from them – the exercise of eating. To remedy this a dog should be given bones from the butcher (preferably beef) which will exercise the dog's jaws and help to keep his teeth sharp and healthy. Equally important, a good bone will keep him contented and happy for hours, often day after day.

The social life of the pack is equated with the social life of the family and it is interesting to see the different relationships, and their intensity, that a dog will form with individuals in the family, and to note how each person is greeted after an absence. Some animals will associate mostly with one person, and these are often referred to as 'one-person dogs'. The intensity of the relationship tends to depend very much on the mutual input. An owner that puts a lot into the relationship will become the object of the greatest affection and loyalty. This is also seen to an interesting extent in sheepdogs where the relationship between master and dog may be a spartan friendship with the animal more of a working tool than a loving companion. The dog is still very anxious to please and work for its dominant master.

Relationships with dogs can also be interesting. Dogs soon build up a working relationship or companionship with neighbouring dogs or with the dogs of visiting friends. Exactly what this is depends a lot on the sex, age and also the size of the individuals and their temperaments. Under normal circumstances dogs become quite friendly in time and this can be used to good advantage when exercising them. Communication between dogs depends very much on scent and it is an absolutely fundamental part of a dog's behaviour to sniff another's anal area, and also to investigate the scent deposited in urine and faeces on posts, and so on. It may embarrass you, but a sniffing and scenting session is an integral part of a dog's exercise and protection of his territory. Deprive him of it and you will end up with a very unhappy, maladjusted dog. Your own exclusive area, for example, a house or a garden, your dog will regard as very much its own territory and another dog or strange human being entering it will be challenged. Certain breeds of dog generally unsuitable as pets will even attack. Such are a menace in the domestic situation and should be kept properly restrained. Over a wider area, particularly that regularly used by you and the dog, the dog will generally associate quite placidly with others. Going into completely strange territory, especially where there are other dogs, you will find that most dogs will keep quite close and rely on their master for guidance. They are on another's territory and will need to make submissive gestures to avoid being attacked. These then are some of the ways in which your dog's make-up should influence your approach to his care and welfare. Because of the attachments which they form to individuals and to places, dogs must be regarded as permanent companions, except in very special circumstances.

Cats are essentially solitary animals and their ancestors, the wild cats of Europe and Asia, do not form social groups as adults or associate together except when young or during the breeding season. The cat is essentially an individual that

A cat out hunting

takes care of its own needs. Partly by their nature and partly because of persecution by man, cats in the wild hunt mainly at night although where they are little disturbed can be seen out and about during the day. In a pet cat the urge to be out and active at night varies between individuals and according to how they are looked after. Pet cats may roam over quite a large area and may form attachments elsewhere as well as with their home base. In the wild a cat will hunt when it is hungry and then rest when this need has been met. In the course of their hunting cats receive all the exercise they need to keep them fit. Even domestic cats get most of their exercise through their instinct to hunt, and many cats, no matter how well they are fed, will still go hunting for birds and small mammals which they will bring home, often untouched.

This is probably an instinctive action to build up a reserve of food when it is available in excess of immediate needs. A similar pattern of behaviour is seen in foxes, who also establish caches of surplus food. Cats are very much individuals, and a basic part of successful cat keeping is the recognition and acceptance of this individual self-centred nature as the basis of their whole way of life, a marked contrast to the strongly social way of life of the dog.

The dog is a complex social animal which is kept largely unconfined in the normal family situation, so we do not have to design for it total living accommodation as we would have to do for wolves living in a zoo. Not all animals have the social make up for which this kind of freedom is appropriate and the third example I shall take is a group of animals including mice, rabbits and guinea pigs, where an artificial total environment has to be provided. I shall use the guinea pig as an example of this and also refer to the rabbit.

Traditionally, guinea pigs, which are attractive plump little rodents from the grasslands of South America, have been kept in hutches. This follows on the tradition of rabbit keeping where these too were normally kept in a hutch with comparatively little room to move or exercise. This was quite deliberate for rabbits were rarely being kept as pets but were being grown and fattened for food. Until quite recently rabbits were considered a great delicacy, and in the country-side rabbits were trapped and reared on a large scale for food. Myxomatosis put an end to the trade in wild rabbits but we now import large quantities of rabbits from China where they have been reared in intensive conditions solely for meat. Such conditions are quite inappropriate for, and alien to, the basis on which we are prepared to keep animals as pets.

Guinea pigs are sociable animals, but unless a large area is available for them, only one male should be kept with a group of females. A large hutch with divided sleeping and living quarters can be used if you are keeping just one or two, but in any case a combination of an outdoor pen with a hutch properly constructed to keep out bad weather is the preferred arrangement. It is also possible to keep guinea pigs on a free range system but again warm, secure hutch accommodation is essential.

Successful pet keeping depends very much on maintaining the ties between pet and owner and this can be carefully reinforced by the feeding and care of the animals. Guinea pigs and rabbits are essentially plant feeders but, because the supply of plant food varies round the year, it is a good idea to use a proprietary pellet food mixture as the basic diet to which is added a variety of vegetables and wild plants in season. One must, however, be careful not to feed too much of anything new. Choice titbits fed by hand, such as a slice of apple or carrot that is not part of the regular daily ration, will greatly help in keeping your pet tame and easy to handle. Guinea pigs and rabbits are the food of predatory mammals and birds such as foxes and buzzards. When out grazing, which they will spend a great deal of time doing, or just sunbathing, they are alert for predators and when alarmed will flee to their burrows. In the outside run situation it is essential that a feeling of security is provided for the animals by providing them with secure places to run to. The social structure of guinea pigs and rabbits is not quite as complex as that of the carnivores and less special provision has to be made for them. They are, however, sociable and it is necessary to ensure that the group does not become too large and that there are not too many males present. In the wild it will often be only immature males that will be tolerated by adult males and the attitude to them adopted by both adult males and females becomes increasingly aggressive so that eventually many of them will leave the area where they were reared. In captivity they are unable to escape from this sort of aggression and have to be removed, and this can also happen with females when numbers become too large. A male guinea pig is rarely aggressive to immature and adult females and can usually be left within the breeding enclosure.

When breeding, however, it is essential to make sure that there are enough sleeping and breeding quarters to go round so that the animals can choose appropriate quarters for

26

themselves. Individual temperaments vary considerably and, while most will get on very amicably together, there are females who do not mix well and a close eye should be kept on the group to make sure that all is well. Buck rabbits (males) are noted for their aggressive tendencies and some females also leave a lot to be desired as regards their temperament. Although the buck may be left to run with the does many breeders prefer to keep the buck separately and to put the female in with him only when ready to be mated. This ensures that the buck does not attack the young, or upset the female. It is something that has to be worked out in practice, for your own animals. Both guinea pigs and rabbits play, and in the wild make use of all sorts of natural features to add variety and complexity to their games. A flat lawn offers little variety and a great deal of stimulus to play can be given by introducing natural obstacles such as rocks and pieces of tree trunk or branches. The introduction of items is necessary because in most cases a movable pen will be used on a lawn rather than a permanent enclosure. One natural instinct of the rabbit that will need to be thwarted is the desire to dig burrows. In some cases this urge may not be so strong and some well built boxes and a few pieces of drain pipe may settle it. A tame rabbit, however, can be a great digger and is capable of tunnelling a considerable distance underground. This is normally prevented by flooring the portable run with wire mesh.

Many of the small birds commonly kept as pets such as budgerigars, zebra finches and parakeets are sociable birds and, in the wild, fly around in quite large flocks. Close personal bonds develop between individual birds and, if conditions are right they will pair up and breed. The conditions needed and the social behaviour vary greatly between different species of birds and the needs of each must be carefully studied in planning your set up. One cannot generalise about this.

In research establishments and laboratories, species commonly used for research studies are kept in intensive accommodation designed for ease of management and hygiene. The

Rabbits in the wild

space provided for each animal is judged to be acceptable by bodies such as UFAW (Universities Federation for Animal Welfare) who are professionally concerned with animal welfare. Certainly, for the commonly kept species such as mice, rats, rabbits and guinea pigs, the animals are fit and well and will produce and rear young. Most people would, however, not wish to keep their pets in such close confinement.

The third method of keeping a pet is one where its natural environment is transferred almost without change into the captive situation. The best example of such keeping is a tank of pond life where it is quite a simple matter to set up the tank and arrange it in such a way that it closely resembles the natural setting. The important thing to remember with a pond life tank is that each species in that ecosystem has its own preferences as to where it lives and this variety and complexity must be provided. There are those that will scavenge on the bottom amongst mud, sand or gravel, depending on the type of pond or stream. Some species will anchor themselves to stones or vegetation while others will

Collecting pond life

spend much of the time underneath stones, like the water scorpion, or concealed amongst the weed like caddis fly larvae, or the carnivorous water beetle nymphs that ambush their prey. Species that live in still water ponds will generally do quite well in an aquarium of sufficient size but those that live in running water will probably not live in an aquarium unless the qualities of running water can be reproduced. This generally means a clear, well oxygenated water supply that can usually be maintained by a filtration and aeration system though, for some, an actual circulation of water will have to be produced by means of a pump. In a larger set up out of doors, it is possible to create a very attractive series of pools embodying all these requirements. Two fibreglass pools can be set up, one higher than the other. A pump takes water from the lower pool via a filter to the upper pool and the overflow is allowed to run down a cascade chute into the lower pool creating a system of clear, circulating, oxygenated water. Oxygenation can also be achieved with the aid of a fountain.

When thinking about creating a pond life set up the main lesson is to look carefully at the habitat from which you are going to collect and to set up your tank accordingly. The essence of the pond life project is its basic simplicity and inexpensiveness. It is, for example, possible to create suitable conditions in just a clean plastic washing up bowl, the advantage of a glass or plastic aquarium only being that you get better all round vision.

There are some basic types of accommodation that form a series of cages in which the principles of construction and design of the basic structure are much the same, although the dimensions are different for each species. It should also be remembered that one can give more space to an animal than the basic minimum so that if you think you might want to keep more of the species, you might decide to build a larger cage or enclosure in the first place. As with the larger cages and runs for the bigger animals, there are also basic designs for smaller animals that can be adapted in various ways. A glass aquarium tank with water in can be used for fish, it can be planted up to keep insects, or furnished for small mammals, reptiles or amphibians simply by making some basic changes. It is the furnishing of the basic cage or enclosure that adapts it to the particular needs of each animal. In the chapters about each pet species details are given of the needs of each animal.

With an outdoor run decide whether it is to be readily portable, for example to be moved every day, or a more permanent fixture. If it is a pen for guinea pigs and rabbits this will normally be a grazing enclosure so you will want to move it frequently. In this case a simple playpen type construction with an open top is desirable. For rabbits though, you may wish to have a wire mesh floor so that they can graze the grass but not dig their way out. If it is a flight cage for birds, or a cage for squirrels, ferrets or similar creatures, a permanent construction and site may be preferred. In this case the framework will need to be strong and will require an access door so that the ground can be cleaned and treated. A permanently sited cage can have its main supports driven into the ground and the framework of the cage fixed to them. There is, however, a lot to be said for constructing any cage on a sectional system so that the various panels and components are simply bolted together. The advantages here are that a sectional cage can be extended or modified quite easily and is very simple to transport if you have to move house or even if you just want to change the site.

An important feature of any cage or enclosure is that it not only keeps your animals in but other animals out. Both dogs and cats may harass guinea pigs and rabbits and although shelters within the enclosure will provide protection this may not be enough. For this reason you may prefer to have the pen roofed with wire mesh as well as the sides. Rats, stoats, weasels and possible foxes can also be a problem and all of these are likely to be encountered at one time or another. Rats will not only take food but will also kill and eat young animals and sometimes adults as well. They, and mice, also harbour and spread various diseases. These predators are often active when you will not be out and about and it is for this reason that most owners will shut their animals in at night in a more durable and stronger house which has carefully been made to keep the predators out.

You will need to have access both to outdoor cages and runs and also into any house. This may be necessary in special situations and for routine treatments when the individuals have to be caught or just for normal handling and cleaning. The most appropriate type of access will depend on the size of the run or hut. With a largeish hut such as those used for aviaries a normal shed-type door giving full height access is usual. A useful modification can be made to this pattern by using a stable door so that the upper half of the door can be opened and fastened back for ventilation. With such a system however, it is advisable to have an inner wire frame door that will keep animals both in and out as necessary while still maintaining ventilation. With smaller hutches and similar box-like accommodation a roof that lifts off or is hinged so that it can be fully opened is desirable so that all parts can be cleaned. In the case of the traditional rabbit hutch, an opening front is preferable to an opening top as it is easier for regular cleaning and feeding.

Access to a large rectangular flight cage is best provided by a full-height door in one side. With any cage of this type, though, it is a great help to have a double door to prevent birds or mammals escaping. Access to the portable cages with sloping sides is best obtained by having one whole side or a section of the side hinged so that it can be opened.

For small cages such as those for mice or hamsters, it is possible to buy ready made cage fronts. These are produced principally for bird fanciers to make their own cages with but are also very suitable for the small mammals. An important feature when building cages, especially those for mammals and strong-billed birds such as parrots, is the choice of material. Although in some ways wood is more satisfactory in that it is a warmer material and easy to work, it has the great disadvantage of being easily gnawed and chipped away to the extent that the animal may gnaw its way out. It is for this reason and also for hygienic purposes that special plastic and metal cages are very widely used. With the larger aviary type cages this problem can be overcome by putting the wire mesh on the inside rather than the outside of the wooden frame-work and ensuring that the mesh is carried over the wood. Gnawing at wood is useful in controlling growth of the teeth in rodents and it is important to ensure that pieces of wood and bone are provided for this purpose. Likewise with birds, particularly parrots, if these show signs of damaging the wood it may be caused by boredom and this can be counter-acted by providing more complex cage fittings and also pieces of wood on which any destructive urges can be spent without damage to the aviary.

Animals living outside need protection from strong sun and chilling breezes. An area of the enclosure is required that will be shaded whatever the position of the sun and a wind break should be effective against wind from any direction. The easiest way to provide against both elements is to build a cross-shaped wall of wood or stone and to partly roof over the area enclosed. The roof provides protection when the sun is very high in the sky. If hutches are provided within the enclosure a useful area of shade will be obtained by raising them off the ground.

An important feature of any cage large or small is adequate ventilation without excessive draught. The best way to ensure this, particularly with the smaller cages, is to use a large area of wire mesh in the construction together with small additional ventilator panels if necessary. Glass aquarium tanks are often used for small mammals and reptiles and for both the correct temperature and humidity are important and ventilation must be provided. In general it may be sufficient if the top of the tank is covered with wire mesh. It should not be covered with a solid material such as wood or glass as the ventilation will be quite inadequate and the animals will probably die. For some tropical species of amphibian and some other animals which require a high humidity then a raised glass top with only a small area left for ventilation will be required. This is a specialist matter, however, and you will need expert guidance before starting to keep such animals. Aquarium tanks are available made of both glass and plastic. Glass ones are to be preferred for most purposes as they do not scratch as readily as the plastic ones and mammals will not gnaw their way out as they easily can from the plastic ones. Plastic tanks are, however, less expensive and are very suitable for short term use with fish, pond life, and so on.

3 Looking after your pet

Food and feeding

The correct feeding of your pet is essential to his fitness and overall health. The type of food used, the amount and the frequency with which it is given are all things which are important to his well being. The food that you give will need to make up a balanced diet. By that we mean that a diet containing the right amounts and proportions of the various things that make up our food. For growth, maintenance of the different parts of the body and to provide protection against disease, your pet, like you, needs *proteins*, *vitamins* and *minerals*. To provide energy the body requires *carbohydrates* and *fats*. The bulk of the food that we eat consists of the protein and carbohydrate elements but most foods contain some of the other items and it is clearly essential that we choose suitable foods for our pet that will give him this balance.

At first it is not always easy to guess what foods will provide this overall balance. One cannot feed a dog or cat, for example, on meat alone because it lacks many of the essential minerals for good bone growth and body maintenance and protection. In the wild almost all meat-eating animals also eat some plants and fruit which helps to provide this balance, and they also gnaw bones to obtain additional minerals. In captivity we have to make the correct choice for our pet as, in most cases, it will not be free to seek other kinds of foods. In the wild an animal knows the sort of balance that is required and actively seeks anything that is lacking from its regular diet.

The food value and the substances present in plants vary throughout the year and most animals have learned how to cope with this variation by shifting to other plants and food sources at different times of the year. Also, most of the plant eaters have evolved a life cycle that fits in with these changes in both the quantity and the quality of the food.

When we have decided the correct type and amounts of food to give our pet we have to decide in what form we are going to provide it. Basically this becomes a choice between a factory made food, such as tinned dog meat and dog biscuit, or the food in its raw form, in this case fresh meat and bone and vegetables and cereals. It is also possible to feed a mixture of the two. If the correct choice is made and both are properly prepared, then there is no difference in food value between commercial and home-made food. The real choice lies in a combination of cost and convenience in giving the feed. To feed a dog fresh meat and the other essentials may be difficult if one does not have ready access to a supply of meat at a reasonable price or a freezer in which to keep larger quantities bought in bulk. In the larger towns many pet shops stock fresh meat and some butchers, especially in the country areas, also produce a very good meat pack for dogs which utilises the waste meat and offal. This is not always available and, failing this, one can choose between feeding tinned dog meat and a commercial biscuit meal, a complete dried meat type food, or a blended complete dog food. Most dogs will find any of these palatable and, over several weeks, you will see if, for any reason, one of them does not suit and whether any additions are necessary. It is important to realise that every ingredient in a feedstuff costs money and that generally you will not be getting the same nutritive value from a food costing much less than another. You may also find that a particular brand does not suit your pet.

With plant feeders like the guinea pig and rabbit you will be able to provide much of their food from the green plants that you can gather from the fields and hedgerows and those that they can graze for themselves from the lawn. Too much green food can cause digestive upsets and a bowl of dry food (oats, bran, maize, brown bread, etc.) should always be available. In autumn and winter the food value of green plants, even if they are still present, will have changed greatly and you will need to give other food. Through the year it is generally helpful if you feed the kinds of vegetables that are in season, and you can also add bread. At any time of year it is also a good idea to give other tasty vegetables and fruit such as carrot and apple as a regular titbit to encourage contact with you. Commercially produced foods are also available for guinea pigs, rabbits and mice. These have, in general, been produced as a complete food for use in feeding laboratory and commercial farm stock. They are completely balanced food made to a very high standard. I have used these over the years for a variety of animals and all have found them palatable and they have kept the animals in absolutely tip-top condition. Because of their quality and convenience I would suggest including some of these foods as a part of the normal diet. The foods generally come in a pelleted form and can be bought by the sack or, in many cases, loose by the pound from a pet store. The sacked food keeps for a long period and is easy to store. Another important feature of the commercial pellet foods is that they are germ and disease-free when delivered. On a number of occasions at an establishment I know they occasionally failed to order enough of the bulk food and bought in a small amount from a local pet shop. On every occasion that this was done disease broke out in the colony because the food was contaminated from the not-so-healthy stock in the pet shop. For this reason it pays to be careful where you buy your animal food. If at all possible buy from a shop that does not keep large quantities of pets in close proximity to the food, especially if conditions do not look as good as they might be. The pelleted feed will be especially valuable during the winter and is not very expensive then compared to the price of vegetables at your local shop. A useful tip is to try and buy things like carrots and swedes by the sack. These are very much cheaper that way and they keep for a long time in a cool place. Your local greengrocer will probably help you, as will a local market trader.

These people are worth cultivating as you can often get cabbage and cauliflower trimmings from them and also damaged fruit that would otherwise go to waste. But do not go mad and feed your pets masses of one thing at a time. (I shall say more about this below.) Remember to keep the balance going. One further advantage of the pellet food is the fact that you can feed it from hoppers. This is a self-feeding system which enables you to leave several days' supply of food for your pet.

There is a tremendous variety of birds, each of which has its own special needs and tastes in food. Large numbers of birds are kept as pets and specialist breeders and zoos have worked out suitable diets for practically every kind. You will certainly have no problem in finding and obtaining the right kind of food for your particular bird. For seed eating birds it is possible to buy from a good pet store as well as by mail order from specialist suppliers, the main range of seeds such as millet, hemp and sunflower. One can also buy by the packet or have made up to order various mixtures of the different kinds of seeds. With the commercially bought trade packet of bird seed it will pay to watch carefully just what your bird eats of the mixture provided. The same comment also applied to similar mixtures sold for hamsters and gerbils. Find out what your pet is eating from the mixture and then go along to your local shop where you should be able to buy each variety of seed loose by itself and make up your own mixture to suit your pet. You will find it very much cheaper. Some of these birds will also enjoy a titbit or two so check out the sort of things they might also like from another breeder or book and also from your own experiments.

Some birds have a more varied diet and it is simpler to provide this from a specialist blended feed than to try and find all the separate constituents yourself. A mynah bird is a good example of a very mixed feeder, and ours were kept in top condition by a basic complete diet produced specifically for mynah birds by a national manufacturer of specialist feeds. This would have been a sufficient food in itself, but the bird took great pleasure from the additional supply of fresh apple, orange, banana and mealworms when these were available.

Fish are mostly fed on commercially produced foods. These are complete foods in themselves and different varieties are available for different species of fish although a single branded food will generally be adequate for all the commonly kept varieties of fish. A fish dealer will be able to advise you on the food when you buy your stock. As with other animals some variety is generally enjoyed and is beneficial. This can be supplied by commercially packed delicacies or by live food, the most common of which are daphnia (water fleas) and also redworms and tubifex worms. These are simply added to the aquarium water and the fish seek them out as they would in the wild.

Much more difficult to feed in captivity are reptiles such as snakes and lizards, and also amphibians like frogs and toads. Snakes and some of the larger reptiles feed by catching live prey such as mice and insects, and in captivity they are notoriously difficult to get settled in and feeding. They feed at comparatively long intervals and it may also be difficult to get them used to feeding on freshly killed food. These animals are only for the most experienced and dedicated pet keepers and they should not be kept by beginners or without seeking considerable advice and assistance beforehand. The fruit eating lizards are less difficult to feed but those lizards, frogs and toads which feed on insects are more difficult. To ensure an adequate supply of food it is necessary to breed maggots, bluebottle flies and mealworms to ensure a regular supply, especially during the winter. Alternatively, these can be bought from specialist suppliers and breeders but they are not cheap. In the summer frogs and toads can be fed insects and other creepy crawlies from the garden. If, however, they do not settle to feed in captivity they (the native ones only, that is) should be released back into the wild at the correct time of year, before autumn sets in.

The frequency with which animals are fed is also important. Some species, particularly the grass eaters, spend the greater part of the day grazing and this pattern is followed by horses, sheep, guinea pigs and rabbits. These species require a comparatively large volume of food which has a relatively low nutritive value in comparison to its actual bulk. A substantial throughput of the natural vegetation is necessary to obtain sufficient nourishment. In these species periods of grazing alternate with periods of rest and, in the cud-chewing animals, the gathered food is regurgitated, chewed and swallowed again. These cud chewers have a large four-chambered stomach into which the gathered vegetation goes largely unchewed. The feeding periods fill this rapidly and the food is then properly chewed and digested when the animal is at rest. In contrast the horse has only a small single-chambered stomach and the food must be thoroughly chewed before being swallowed. For this reason the greater part of a horse's day is taken up with feeding. The period spent eating can, however, be greatly reduced by feeding much more concentrated foodstuffs such as horse and pony cubes or cereals such as bruised oats. These may only take a few minutes to eat. Other animals, in particular the carnivores, are used to eating a single large meal after a period of rapid activity (hunting) which they follow by a long period of rest. Because food gathering plays such a fundamental part in the way of life and wellbeing of the animal, it is important to try and match the feeding pattern in captivity. Too little time spent gathering food will result in insufficient exercise, too much rest and the animal perhaps becoming overweight. It is also likely to be reflected in boredom which may express itself in various ways – perhaps greater aggression towards other individuals, damage to the cage and its fittings, abnormal behaviour patterns, feather pecking and fur biting.

If you are able to leave your rabbit or guinea pig to graze for much of the time this system in unlikely to lead to any problems and a single feed of special food and extras can, if necessary, be given as an additional meal. If it is to be fed on more concentrated foods then several small feeds should be given spread through the day.

Meat eaters in particular will suffer if they are not regularly exercised and they will thrive as adults on a single large meal a day after which they will want to sleep. For this reason it makes sense to feed your dog about an hour before his last brief toilet exercise so that he can retire to bed comfortable on a full stomach.

In the wild, birds spend a great deal of time feeding and if they are not able to follow this pattern you are likely to have behavioural problems. In practice the best way to feed the bird is to provide feeding points containing the principal food, but, in the case of seed eaters, it is better to scatter some of a favourite seed over the ground amongst the grass, so that they have to seek it out grain by grain. This is especially recommended for birds such as chickens and pheasants who also, kept under these more natural conditions, will seek out plenty of green food and insects to supplement their basic feed. Insect-eating birds such as mynahs will also spend hours hunting for mealworms or maggots scattered around. The same method has also been employed in many zoos to counteract boredom amongst monkeys who, in the wild, again spend a great deal of time gathering a considerable variety of food, much of it very small. Mealworms or grains of wheat are scattered amongst the peat or sawdust lining in the cage.

It is rarely realised just how much effort is required to obtain the daily supply of energy. Part of the food of the red squirrel is the seeds of the Scots pine which are embedded deep in the cone. Each seed weighs about 0.001 of a gram and each cone contains about 0.1g of seed. Now, an adult squirrel requires about 100g of food per day so that each day it would have to process something like a thousand cones, a considerable time and energy-consuming activity if eating only pine seeds. In practice, of course, a range of other seeds are taken and in captivity it would be given a variety of substitute foods such as nuts and fruits which would supply its calorific needs in about five minutes.

All animals find security and well-being in familiar surroundings, activities and regularity. Your pet will very soon become accustomed to the routines of the family and it will be important that you keep to as close a timetable as possible for feeding, cleaning and handling. You will find that your pet is actively looking for your presence at a particular time and, if it is used to being exercised or handled, will come to expect this at the same time each day. Even, therefore, if you are in a hurry, do follow your regular routine however briefly it must be on that particular occasion. Regularity with regard to a timetable of feeding is also important from a health point of view. It is not good for an animal to be fed irregularly or to have to wait overlong for its food. In some animals it can cause severe upset to the digestive system.

The pattern of feeding that you actually adopt for your pet can expect to change with time, especially if you are starting with a youngster. These nearly always need more frequent feeding and different foods to those they will need as adults. Similarly, pregnant animals will need extra food of high quality to provide all the extra nutriment needed by the babies inside and the same applies for a mother feeding young—additional foodstuffs and a greater frequency of feeding. As you change towards the adult pattern of feeding it makes sense to adapt this towards a timetable that will fit in with the family routine. We have mentioned feeding dogs in the late evening, and this is also a time that offers most families the chance to spend some time with their pet. Routine care of guinea pigs and rabbits should involve you in checking and feeding them before you go to school and again when you have come home, when you will also probably need to clean them out as well. You should also stick to this timetable during the school holidays and at weekends, even if they get extra attention then. It is very wrong of you to feed them regularly at half-past-seven in the morning during schooltime and then expect them to wait till ten o'clock while you have a sleep in! All animals, fish, birds, reptiles and mammals respond to and benefit from a regular regime of feeding and management.

The amount of food that you give is important to your pet's health. You will need to provide it with all the different kinds of foodstuffs necessary for its well-being and sufficient energy foods for its activities. Obviously these vary between species and also between individuals. Young animals have relatively greater needs than do adult animals, and pregnant or lactating mothers need greater amounts of nutriment all round, as well as specific substances in relatively greater amounts. The basic nutriments and their approximate amounts are fairly easy to judge, but it is the energy foods, the fats and carbohydrates, that need to be judged and varied more carefully. These need to be enough for the energy needs of your pet and will obviously vary with the amount of exercise being taken. Too much food or insufficient activity means that the surplus is turned into fat. It is unfortunate that a great many domestic animals are grossly overweight and it is no kindness to have them in this condition. As in humans, obesity causes health problems and puts additional strain on the body. Your pet's carbohydrate intake should be adjusted so that in your overall regime it retains its figure and fitness. You will have to judge the actual amounts for yourself by trial and error. With pregnant or nursing animals, and also to some extent with growing ones, it is desirable to feed according to your pet's appetite. Often, then, your pet is the best guide to its own food needs.

Certain species have a natural mechanism within the body whereby in times of plenty (generally in the summer and autumn) they build up a reserve of food in the form of fat in the body. Animals which do this include horses, deer, dormice, squirrels, badgers and hedgehogs. This reserve of fat is used to help them survive the winter period when, in the wild, they would probably not be able to find sufficient food each day to keep them going by topping up whatever food they have been able to obtain. In the natural pattern of things these reserves would have been used up by the spring. If your pet shows signs of following this pattern it may be upset by not being able to feed *ad lib* and to lay down its fat. If you do allow it to feed *ad lib*, which I think is a good idea as long as it it does not get too overweight, then during the winter you must help it to use up this fat reserve by restricting the amount of food which you supply. This restriction should only apply to energy foods (which is what fat is) and not to proteins, vitamins and minerals which are vital for health and body maintenance rather than energy supply. Not doing this can result in very considerable problems the following year when fattening starts all over again.

You yourself would not buy stale food, particularly meat, fish or vegetables to prepare for your family, for the obvious reason that they have lost most of their food value and could well make you ill. Exactly the same applies to the food which you buy for your pet. You will only get value for money and keep your pet well if you buy food of good quality and freshness. You may, of course, be given damaged fruit or green trimmings such as the outside leaves of cauliflower. These are acceptable and can be used as long as you sort them through and cut out the bruised or damaged parts of the fruit and any bruised or frosted leaves. Vegetables that have been damaged by frost – and a lot of those on sale during the winter have been damaged – are very dangerous and can easily prove fatal for rabbits and guinea pigs in particular.

You should take care in both the preparation and presentation of your pet's food. The principal meals which you give should be served up in appropriate containers so that they will not be spoilt and wasted by being trampled on. Any perishable food not consumed (e.g. meat and vegetables) should not be left beyond the next meal. This does not, of course, apply to dry seeds and pellet foods or cereals such as oats and flake maize provided this has not been soiled. Do be careful, however, if your pet will not eat one of these foods which it normally consumes readily. This refusal is often the first indication that your pet is not well or it can mean that the food has become tainted, for example, by mice. Hygiene is very important and, where a water bowl and a feeding bowl are being used, it is a good idea to have two sets. The set not in use is first washed and then put to soak in a bucket of Milton, which is a mild steriliser that will kill germs and bacteria without tainting the dish for subsequent food. All food should be prepared fresh, particularly some fruits like apples which go brown once they have been cut up.

Where seed is being fed to birds, feed hoppers are the most

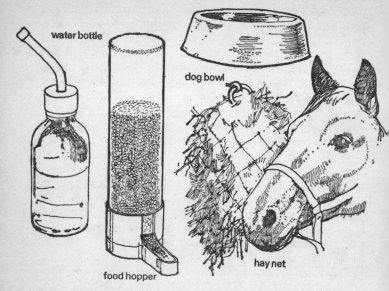

water bottle

dog bowl

food hopper

hay net

Food and water containers for different pets

convenient and for the smaller bird these clip on to the outside of the cage. With larger birds, such as bantams or pheasants, and bigger aviaries, the seed or pellet food can be put in a much larger free-standing self-dispensing hopper which will also keep the contents dry. Similar hoppers can be used for free-range guinea pigs and rabbits. Bowls are not very good for many of these animals as they tend to sit in the dish or perch on the side, which can result in a lot of spoilage. When feeding hay, bulk greens or cereals to almost any kind of animal be it a rabbit, guinea pig, pony or calf, you will save yourself a great deal of food and money if you present the food in a raised trough or rack. Hay or greens fed on the ground get trampled on and will not be eaten. Using a rack or a haynet hung from above, the animal only takes a mouthful at a time. Chickens, for example, enjoy greenstuffs and may be given cabbage stalks hung in the run so that the birds get the full benefit of them.

Earlier in this chapter I mentioned the problem of boredom for those animals that normally spend a great deal of time and effort in gathering their own food. If the situation allows, you can encourage your pet to forage for some of his food by scattering small pieces of favoured titbits round the run. This is particularly to be recommended where hard seeds and pellets are involved though the latter should not be scattered if the ground is wet or rain is likely as they will disintegrate. Scattered food should, as far as possible, be used to counteract boredom between meals. In keeping chickens this method is particularly recommended when, during the day, the birds forage for themselves and a few handfuls of scattered corn keeps them near by. At night they are normally fed a hot mash which supplies additional nutrients, gives them a warm meal which they look forward to before going to roost and ensures that you can get them in easily to shut them up for the night.

For many species the range of food given will change very little through the year but in others, particularly the plant feeders, summer produces a much greater possible variety of food and a surplus of such things as lettuce. One must be very careful how any change in the diet is made and in the quantity of anything new that is given. Digestive systems do not cope well with a sudden excess of something new or with a rapid overall change, say, from pellets and roots to grass or leafy greens. In nature, changes take place gradually and new foods are present at first in only small amounts so that the body gets used to their presence. If you make sudden changes your pet is likely to get ill. Give only small amounts of a new plant at first and increase it slowly bearing in mind that it should form only a part of a balanced diet.

Water has no nutritive value but it is an essential part of every living thing and your animals will need it. Some need more than others and get their water in different ways. In the wild animals may get their water directly by drinking from pools and streams or by licking rain and dew from plants. Some animals such as hamsters and gerbils which come from desert countries have become very efficient at conserving water and in the wild for much of the time can survive on the water that is produced within their bodies by the chemical breakdown of various foodstuffs. There are very few animals that can do this and even these species should have access to water although they will not drink very much. Animals that are eating large amounts of moist foods like leaves, grasses and fruits that contain a lot of water will need less than the same species living on a commercial pellet diet or on roots. In hot weather most animals will need more water to replace that which they lose as perspiration or in the case of dogs, by panting. Water is necessary as a part of most of the processes that go on in the body and for the removal of waste substances in urine is very important. Carnivores in particular, because of their meat diet, need plenty of water to keep their bodies functioning properly and to remove waste products which would otherwise be likely to accummulate in and cause damage to the kidneys. It must be a fundamental rule of keeping almost every pet that they have access at all times to a good quantity of fresh water. In the case of dogs and cats this is often given in a deep bowl refilled several times a day so that it can be lapped up. For birds a water hopper is particularly useful. For most other mammals neither the bowl nor the hopper is very satisfactory as small mammals are inclined to defecate in bowls and to gnaw at hoppers, so that they cease to work. The most satisfactory system consists of an inverted bottle which has a metal tube with a teat-like end passing through the stopper. All animals readily learn to use this kind of vessel and to suck water from it. Bottles of various sizes can be purchased so that, if absolutely necessary, several days' supply can be provided. Nearly all water containers in regular use develop a growth of algae if they are not regularly cleaned and sterilised. Dirty water bottles are also one of the most effective ways of passing on germs to your pets. As mentioned, the water vessels should be sterilised daily and the inside of the bottle scrubbed out with a bottle brush.

If you are gathering wild food for your pets be careful where you are getting it from. Make sure that the plants have not been sprayed with a plant killer or insecticide or been

Scattering corn around the run makes chickens forage for their food, counteracting boredom

given some other treatment during growth. Another major source of plant food that needs to be treated with caution is a roadside verge. Any roadside verge tends to have rather dirty vegetation from the dust kicked up by passing cars, which is not good for your animals. More serious though, especially to young animals, is the presence of fine particles of other harmful substances in this dust, or substances which may have been taken up by the plants themselves. The most important of these are contamination by lead from petrol fumes, and particles of rubber and paint used in road marking. If at all possible, avoid gathering food from the roadside.

Another source of lead poisoning that has only recently been appreciated is that from lead shotgun pellets in animals such as rabbits which have been shot as food for meat-eating animals such as birds of prey, foxes and ferrets. The small particles of shot which are often spread through the body of the food animal separate in the predator's stomach and often remain there. These then gradually dissolve releasing lead, which is a very poisonous substance, into the bloodstream causing severe and progressive illness.

Finally, you may occasionally see examples of what we call depraved appetite, when your pet starts eating all manner of odd things or gnawing at wood or metal. This is an indication that all is not well and it can be caused by a lack of something in the food, or an illness. One of the commonest causes is the lack of a trace element or substance in the diet and this can be easily remedied by giving a mineral supplement. The behaviour is often quite specific for dietary deficiencies and certain animals are known to have a tendency to show particular conditions. The other cause may be due to the presence of internal parasites, and again a good book on your particular pet will guide you as to its likely cause and whether a proprietary treatment or a visit to the vet is necessary.

Care of the coat

The outer covering of your pet, whether it is of feathers, fur or scales, must be kept in good condition, and although most animals take extremely good care of their coats it may be necessary for you to provide the means for them to do this and also to do some of it for them. Wild animals are well able to take care of their own coats and spend much of the day cleaning and grooming their fur or feathers. A number of the varieties of pets that we have bred, such as long-haired dogs, cats, and guinea pigs cannot cope naturally with their long hair and occasionally you will find a pet animal that is not as careful as it should be. With these animals regular brushing and combing of the coat will be necessary to keep it free of tangles. A lot depends on the variety of pet that you have just how often you should brush its coat. A long-haired Afghan hound or a Persian cat is likely to require attention twice a day whereas most dogs and cats will benefit from, but not necessarily need, a grooming session once a day. One of my own dogs, a Border Collie/Spaniel loves exploring in deep vegetation and frequently comes out with her coat full of twigs, burrs and sticky 'sweethearts'. It takes her about two hours to sort them out but we often do it for her. Regular grooming is a great benefit to your pet dog or cat. It helps to keep the fur clean of particles of dirt, parasites and scurf and gives the fur a good sheen and lustre. If you are showing your dog then a daily grooming session will be part of your routine preparation for showing.

Most mammals will, from time to time, pick up external parasites such as fleas and ticks and a regular part of coat maintenance can be a dusting with an appropriate killer or the use of an insecticidal shampoo. If your dog or cat is regularly found to have fleas they may also be present in the house although you would be largely unaware of this. There are periodic outbreaks of animal fleas in houses but these can be dealt with simply and without embarrassment with advice from your Public Health Office.

No amount of grooming or treatment will make a coat look good if the animal is not in good condition. The coat will only be in tip-top shape if the right food is provided, so a coat that does not lie well and looks dull and lifeless is usually a sure sign that something is lacking. Commonly this is a specific

Dogs should be groomed regularly, especially long-haired varieties like this English Setter

vitamin deficiency and can be remedied with cod-liver oil. All animals may need the occasional supplement such as this especially in the winter when sunshine is limited, but if the need for a supplement does arise you should take a careful look at your basic feeding.

For grooming you should have a completely separate set of brushes and combs that are kept especially for that purpose. You should especially not use them yourself. You should keep them clean and not use them on other animals until you have cleaned them to avoid passing on parasites and infections. Remember that many skin parasites and their eggs are so small that you would hardly notice them with the naked eye unless you searched very carefully with a magnifying glass.

Grooming must be carried out with care because sometimes you may be removing much of the natural oil and scurf in the coat that is part of the animal's protection against the weather. This is especially true of horses and ponies where the wrong kind of grooming can remove most of the animal's natural weatherproofing which results in it becoming damp and chilled. The requirements of a working animal and one that lives or works outside for much of the time are, of course, rather different than for purely indoor pets, so do make sure you get expert advice about the needs of your particular animal.

At least once a year and often more frequently your pet will moult his hair, fur or feathers. Some species do it rapidly at a particular time of year whilst in others it can be a rather more drawn-out business. It is important that the moult be recognised for what it is and not be considered as something wrong. Fur and feathers consist principally of protein and therefore at the time of the moult your pet is going to need relatively greater amounts of protein than normal, and it is a good idea to give him some extra. Both birds and animals will assist the moult by rubbing the coat or by pecking at the base of the feathers to loosen them and this is not a sign of skin or parasite trouble. Your mammal will greatly appreciate your assistance in this process with brushing and combing to remove the loose hair.

Good health

Properly cared for your pet should remain healthy for much of its life but there are various things specifically connected with health and hygiene that you should do to help protect it. Our most commonly kept large pets – dogs and cats – can suffer greatly from a number of killer diseases. At one time diseases such as leptospirosis, distemper and feline enteritis killed a great many dogs and cats each year. The diseases were not pleasant, causing a great deal of pain and discomfort to the animal and nearly always proving fatal. Likewise it was very upsetting to lose a pet, often time and time again, because of infections which were rife, and to some extent they are still very much with us, although far fewer dogs and cats suffer nowadays. The reason for this decline in the number of these diseases is because of the development of vaccines against them. Vaccinations are now given routinely to their young animals by all caring pet owners. It does not, however, alter the fact that the diseases are still very much with us and that unprotected animals continue to die from them. For dogs, routine protection against the following diseases can be given: distemper (hard pad), viral hepatitis, kidney leptospirosis and liver leptospirosis; for cats protection can only be given against feline enteritis, perhaps the most virulent of cat diseases, but there is no inoculation for cat flu although this can be treated successfully if caught at an early stage. For horses it is now customary and very advisable to vaccinate against tetanus and influenza. An important reason for vaccinating dogs against leptospirosis is the fact that this disease is transmissable to humans, although the number of cases each year is fortunately low. There are in theory a very considerable number of diseases that are to be found in wild animals that can be transmitted to human beings, and there have been a few very unpleasant outbreaks. A group of animals considered the most dangerous of all is the primates (monkeys, apes and so on) whose diseases are in many cases similar to those found in human beings. Many of these diseases have little effect on the animals themselves but when transmitted to man become highly virulent. Many of these organisms are not well known and treatments are limited. Another disease that can be transmitted to humans is psittacosis (ornithosis) which is typical of the parrot family. Cases are few but the disease is unpleasant. Cross infection of serious disease is very rare from pet animals. The commonly kept pets have been bred in captivity for many generations and have proved to be free of dangerous diseases of their own although they can catch others that have been associated with man and his animals for centuries. The danger comes from exotic pets, many of which were until recently imported directly from the wild. As these are now mostly bred in captivity one can normally expect any health hazard to be detected.

No one wants to believe that their pet is carrying germs or parasites that can harm them but even if you look after your pets really well there is the possibility that they will pick up something and pass it on to you just as you in your wanderings can pick up a virus quite unwittingly and bring it back to them. Pat a strange horse's muzzle, come home and pet that of your own pony and you may well have given it equine influenza. Your dog picks up your shoe, which may well be carrying leptospirosis. Another health hazard from pets particularly dogs and cats, is the transmission of internal parasitic worms. This can largely be avoided by regularly dosing your pet against them. Specific advice is available in specialist books and also in leaflets produced by the major companies concerned in the production of petfoods and medicines, and a regular programme of dosing and care is inexpensive and will cause no discomfort to your pet, in fact quite the contrary, he will be all the better for it.

Minor illnesses or conditions, especially of birds and fish, if they are correctly recognised, can be treated by the owner with special proprietary medicines which can be purchased from a chemist or a pet store. A number of conditions are fairly typical of some species and will be recognised from their description in a good book about that animal. If, however, there is any doubt in your mind as to the nature of the condition or if the animal is in pain or is not responding to a treatment it should be taken to a veterinary surgeon, at once. A veterinary surgeon will also be able to give you advice on caring for your pet and to advise on routine protection and vaccination as well as to treat any particular conditions which arise. If you are buying a kitten or a puppy consult him by telephone about the arrangements for inoculations and so on before taking your pet to the surgery. Veterinary surgeons have a wide experience of illnesses and injuries to pets and have the necessary skill and equipment to treat them. They also have a much greater range of medicines; many of the most effective compounds are not available for sale to the public. Let the vet treat your pet whilst you concentrate on the nursing side.

Responsibility

When you have a pet you have a responsibility to other people to see that it does not cause harm or do damage. This really only applies to the larger pets such as dogs, cats, horses and some of the more unusual ones. Dogs are one of the major causes of road accidents and it is important that you should keep your dog under control and on a lead when taking it out anywhere near traffic. Your dog should be trained to follow your basic commands and help can be obtained with this from local dog training classes. You won't, however, have your dog fully trained until it is about a year old; young dogs take a time to learn the basics. You are required by law to license your dog each year and it is also required to wear a collar with the owner's name and address on it.

Cats are less of a problem and no licence is required for them. Many owners allow their cats to roam freely but would be very upset if your dog went into their garden. I do not like other people's cats roaming into my garden as they dig up plants, catch and frighten birds that we encourage, and also disturb our other animals, but cats enjoy an unreasonable degree of freedom on other people's property compared to most other animals.

If you have a dog, horse or pony or other large animal there is a very real possibility that it could be involved in a road accident. In many circumstances it will be you, the owner of the animal, that is legally responsible for causing the accident. It is advisable that an owner of any of these animals holds a third party liability insurance giving coverage up to £250,000 for any harm caused by their pet. Such insurance is very cheap and is normally available along with other types of insurance policy. In this way if a serious accident results from your pet the people affected can obtain adequate recompense without you and your family losing all their goods to try and meet the damages awarded by a Court.

4 Dogs

The dog was the first animal to be domesticated by man and the earliest domesticated dogs in Europe lived about 9000 years ago. The dog was domesticated from the wolf. Dogs are one of the most popular and most suitable of animals as pets for both individuals and families. They are basically straightforward to take care of, look after themselves and have very few problems associated with them.

Throughout the world there are a great many different kinds of dog – over 300 are recognised. The different kinds of dogs are known as breeds, and differences within a breed such as rough or smooth-haired kinds are known as varieties. The different breeds have been selected over a very long period of time to be suitable for particular purposes. Thousands of years ago the Egyptians kept Greyhounds which they used for hunting gazelles and other animals, and the Assyrians had huge powerful hounds which they used to hunt lions and other large wild game. The breeds have been produced for a great many reasons, so you get some which have particular skills, such as the hounds which are extremely good at following a scent – Greyhounds and Whippets are very fast and are used both for hunting and racing; and gun dogs such as Retrievers which are used to recover shot birds. Others were bred for their coat and for their unusual appearance and may or may not have other useful features. The temperaments and personalities of the different breeds varies considerably, breeds come and go in popularity, and trends within a breed can change. Some dogs are quite unsuitable as family pets, I would place Greyhounds and Foxhounds firmly in

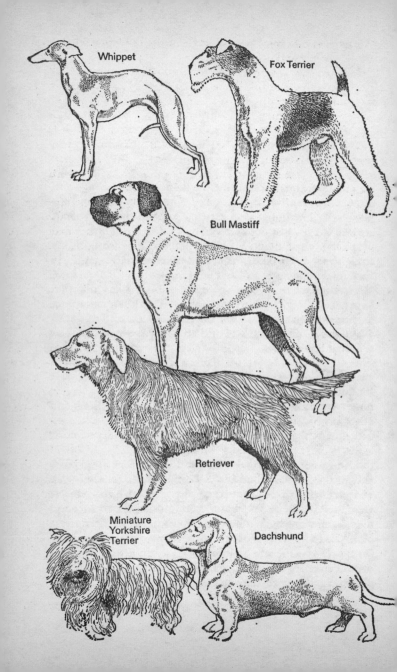

Whippet

Fox Terrier

Bull Mastiff

Retriever

Miniature
Yorkshire
Terrier

Dachshund

this category for most people, but many of the faults are due to the owners and not to the dogs.

When selecting a breed for a family dog temperament is all important and it should be a breed that is of a suitable size for your home and one which can be exercised and looked after within the framework of your family activity. Do not buy on impulse but consider carefully the merits of the breeds which appeal to you, and very important, ask yourself why you really want a dog. Dogs are long-lived animals and barring accidents it is very unlikely that your dog will be with you for anything less than ten years.

Most dogs will share the owner's home rather than be kept in outside accommodation. Outside kennels need to be very carefully constructed to be warm and dry, and heating may also be required. Many breeds should not live outside unless extra warmth is provided. The traditionally drawn kennels are quite unsuitable. Indoors the needs of your dog are very simple. He will require a bed of his own which is best provided as a basket or box with raised sides to keep out draughts with a soft blanket on which to lie. This is better if raised off the floor and positioned so as to be out of draughts and in a reasonably cosy spot. This will be the principal sleeping quarters, though during the day the dog will often choose to lie elsewhere, often where there is a view. Your dog will undoubtedly prefer the sofa, the best armchair, the rug in front of the fire or to sleep on your bed. Dogs are real chancers so from the start be firm about things like this. The only other indoor need is a bowl of fresh water available at all times.

Dogs are carnivores and their principal source of nourishment is derived from meat. In the wild a dog would obtain the whole carcass and in this way would eat a variety of meat together with fat and vegetable matter. Many carnivores also gather fruit as a separate item. Your pet should be fed meat, biscuit and some vegetables, especially greens and carrots. The vegetables are usually available as scraps to be added to the basic meal. The meat provided can be of several kinds. Fresh meat raw or cooked, tinned meat, sheep and cattle

A dog bed

paunch (tripe) or as part of a complete food. Fresh meat has much to recommend it as you know exactly what you are buying. Tinned dog foods vary considerably in their contents, especially in the amount of water, and a detailed analysis is rarely given. Fed to the manufacturers' instructions they do, however, provide a full, nourishing diet. For many families tinned meats or dried meats are very convenient and have the advantage that they can be bought at local shops and supermarkets. The complete feeds certainly do the dogs extremely well and mine have always thrived on them. The particular brand I used was bought in 25kg (56 lb) bags as a dry mixture which was moistened to a porridge-like consistency, and although not looking like one's idea of a dog's dinner, the animals loved it. It is very economically priced and probably has the edge on price over the other alternatives despite their convenience. Though most petshops provide a regular service of good quality meat, there is a fringe of suppliers who attempt to pass off the inferior if not bad meat for pets, sometimes in frozen pack form. If, when offered for sale or when thawed, the meat is not fresh and reasonably appetising to you, look for an alternative supplier. Any of the branded foods can be obtained much more cheaply by buying in bulk either from a local wholesaler or by negotiation with your local store. Pet foods frequently feature in High Street price-cutting operations and you would be well advised to purchase your preferred brands when they are offered as loss leaders and save yourself several pence per tin. Fresh paunch can be obtained from your local abbatoir but normally only on the basis of a regular supply. Paunch is normally cooked and then offered in the same way with biscuit as meat (which it is). It is probably the cheapest form of protein for your dog but it is not the most convenient, especially if you live in a small house or only have a single small dog.

Dogs also like bones, they keep them happy for hours and perform certain very important functions. Aside from providing certain essential minerals their importance lies in the exercise they provide for the jaw muscles, and for the rasping and cleansing which they give to the teeth. Only certain types of bone are suitable, namely the large substantial bones of cattle or horses which are generally known as marrow bones. You can get these from your butcher. The bones of smaller animals like sheep and pigs are smaller and the jaws of most dogs break them and the animals consume them entirely. In such cases the faeces are noticeably firm, white and calcareous looking. They often contain so much bone that archaeologists recover this type of dog faeces from sites thousands of years old. Normally these raw bones will not cause any problems to your dog as they break up into pieces that do no harm *but* cooked bones are very different. When cooked, bones become much more brittle and this means that they often shatter into jagged pieces. The same is

This is the sort of large beef marrow-bone you should give your dog to gnaw

true for the fresh bones of birds and also hares and rabbits. These bones can become wedged in the throat, from which they can generally be removed, but more seriously they can puncture the stomach, intestines or bowel, so do not give your dog these bones. For much the same reason fish bones should also be avoided.

The amount of food to be given to your dog obviously varies with its size and the amount of exercise it is getting. You will need to adjust the quantity fed to keep him in good shape, and do remember that as in humans overweight takes years off the life and puts an extra strain on the heart. In the adult dog a single meal is the normal practice, usually given in the evening to keep the dog contented through the night. A few dog biscuits may be given at one time during the day, often on return from a walk. Do not feed your dog between meals and do not allow him to beg titbits from you or from visitors at mealtimes.

Only a very rough guide can be given as to the quantity of food to be fed, the actual amounts will need to be worked out according to the circumstances and the type of dog. A very small dog weighing under 2.25kg (5 lb) will need about 140g (5 oz) of food a day. The smaller breeds weighing about 11kg (25 lb) will need about 560g (20 oz) and a 22kg (50 lb) dog about 850g (30 oz) One of about 45kg (100 lb), that is one of the larger breeds, will require about 1.3kg (3 lb) of food a day. This should be fed as a mixture of about two-thirds meat to one-third biscuit. Note that the amount of food needed does not increase directly with weight, the larger dogs need proportionately less than the smaller ones.

The feeding regime for a puppy is quite different, involving a variety of foods at more frequent intervals changing as the puppy grows up. For rearing a puppy you take expert advice for the breed and for the type of food being used.

Exercise is vital to a dog for both its physical fitness and also for its psychological well being. The exercise requirements vary with the breed of dog. The very active breeds and sporting dogs such as hounds will need upwards of 16 km (10 miles) a day, though the large but heavier breeds need rather less. Middle-size dogs such as Labradors require a minimum of about 9 km (6 miles) whilst 3–4 km (2–3 miles) will be sufficient for the smaller breeds. About half the total distance needed should be given at a fast pace but do bear in mind the length of your dog's legs and the pace at which they are having to work. The exercise regime and approach is different for puppies and you may also have to modify the working routine for elderly animals. Where exercise has to be reduced some adjustment should be made in the amount of food given to avoid obesity which will further aggravate many of the conditions of old age. The owner will also benefit from the dog's exercise but it is not necessary for him to cover quite the same amount of ground! A dog will obtain fast exercise and cover a great deal more ground when it can play games with its owner or with another dog. Speed exercise can also be given by training the dog to run to heel being led off a bicycle. However, this kind of exercise should only be given on paths and tracks and not on public roads for reasons of safety, and it *must not* be overdone otherwise the dog will be strained. A mixture of walking, playing and running is the basis of a good exercise programme. Dogs enjoy exercise but don't expect an unfit dog to suddenly enjoy a long distance walk or run. If your dog is out of condition introduce him to it gently.

Most dogs take care of their coats but in some species, especially the long-haired ones, this is not so simple and regularly combing and brushing is necessary to keep the coat in good order. How often this is needed depends on the breed and can vary from twice a day in a show Afghan to up to a week. For smooth-haired dogs with no coat problems a weekly grooming is probably all that is necessary (though a daily grooming is desirable) and can form part of a weekly routine inspection of ears, eyes and teeth. It is suggested that a routine examination is made each week so as to spot the early signs of any trouble such as minor cuts or allergies. Dogs do not require regularly bathing in most cases and it is quite unnecessary except in certain special breeds and for some show purposes. Our Labrador and Spaniel are usually given a shampoo bath twice a year using an insecticidal shampoo as a routine precaution. If you do bath your dog, do it on a warm day and make sure he is dried properly afterwards.

Dogs will normally be very healthy animals but are susceptible anywhere in town and country to killer or severely debilitating diseases: hardpad (distemper), viral hepatitis and kidney and liver leptospirosis. These can now be prevented by a routine course of vaccinations as a puppy followed by boosters as an adult. The age at which this is given is quite specific and no responsible dog owner should fail to have the inoculations done.

All dogs can pick up external parasites especially during the summer. Those such as fleas and ticks can be dealt with by dusting with an appropriate insecticidal powder or shampoo. The most suitable depend on the actual problem. All dogs, no matter how well cared for or with whom they live, are affected by internal parasites known as worms. There are two groups, the small threadlike roundworms, and tapeworms. These are controlled by two different medicines given orally. These worming medicines are extremely effective, have no unpleasant side effects and are easy to administer. Dogs should be wormed routinely about three times a year and at any other time that symptoms appear. The commonest indications of worms are a combination of one or more of the following: scratching of the anal region, bottom dragging (because of irritation), bad breath, depraved appetite and the coat lacking lustre. Bottom dragging can, however, be caused by impacted anal glands, a painful condition but one which your vet can deal with simply and effectively. Worms, either the threadlike ones or the little white wriggling envelopes of tapeworms can be seen in the faeces of badly infected animals, but worms can still be present even when they are not visible to the naked eye, and can be passed on to other animals. Your veterinary surgeon will be able to supply you with the correct medicine for both kinds of worm and also the dose and course of treatment to be followed. Proprietary branded medicines that can be sold to the general public over the counter of pet stores are often not as effective as some of the medicines which are only available to the veterinary surgeon to be used on his advice. Many of the newer and most effective treatments are only obtainable through your vet.

You will readily notice when your dog is a bit off-colour – he may suffer from a loss of appetite, wind or bad breath, but often these things will be minor upsets. If the condition persists take your dog to the vet.

There are certain legal requirements that must be met by any dog owner. All adult dogs must be licensed with the Local Authority and this takes the form of a licence issued by your local post office dated and timed to the minute, which will cost you at present 37½p per year. Your dog is also required to wear a collar which carries the name and address of the owner. You also have a responsibility to keep your dog under control and not allow it to be a nuisance. Control of your dog is vital because each year all over the country loose dogs are responsible for thousands of road accidents. You should never allow your dog to be out and about on its own, and anywhere near a road you should have your dog on a lead, however, old and well trained you may think he is. If your dog causes an accident you could be held fully liable for the consequences of that accident. As mentioned in Chapter 3, all owners of large animals would be well advised to have third party liability insurance for all members of the family to cover themselves against the financial consequences of being liable for an accident. As a responsible dog owner you will also keep your dog under control in the countryside or in a city deer park where your dog can be shot on sight if found worrying sheep, deer or other livestock. To farmers on the edge of towns and cities as well as in the countryside dogs worrying livestock are responsible for a lot of damage each year.

To get the most from your dog you will need to train it to obey your instructions and to follow a basic pattern of discipline. Training a dog is not difficult but it does take time and needs to be spread over quite a long period with different things being taught at different ages. It is something that requires a great deal of patience on the part of the owner and also a great deal of personal discipline. Before you attempt to train your dog you should get a book from the library about this basic training so that you appreciate just what is involved and how you go about teaching. All members of the family must learn to use the same commands and to behave properly when giving them especially during the training period. All over the country dog training classes are held and you will find it very helpful to join one of these where an expert trainer is on hand to guide you.

Dogs are best purchased from specialist breeders or

1 *A Connemara pony*

2 Above: *A smooth-haired guinea pig*

3 Below: *The gerbil, a small desert mammal originally from Mongolia, is now a very popular pet*

4 Above: *A Common Lizard, basking*

5 Below: *A European Salamander*

6 Above: *Some wild animals, such as the hedgehog, can be encouraged in the garden*

7 Below: *Wild animals such as this fox cub can make fascinating pets but are only suitable for the really experienced pet keeper*

8 *Blue tits feeding on peanuts*

9 Above: *A Foxhound with her puppies*

10 Below: *The right way to transport your pets*

11 Above: *A hamster getting to know its owner*

12 Below: *Budgerigars in an outdoor aviary*

13 *A cat grooming one of its kittens*

obtained from a dog home if a suitable one is available. I do not like puppies being sold from town pet stores or from people who have allowed their bitch to be mated by accident. Mongrels in themselves are delightful animals in most cases, but anything that encourages irresponsible breeding and sale of puppies is not to be encouraged. You can inspect the stock of different breeders and make up your mind for a particular individual in a litter. You will then be buying on the strength of the breeder's reputation an animal that will be a good example of its kind, and if for any reason this is not the case then you have a comeback on the breeder, who will be anxious to preserve his reputation. You will pay more for a quality puppy than buying from a back street trader but you are, after all, buying a companion for a great many years and the money will be well spent. The price you will pay will depend very much on the popularity of the breed and the reputation of that breeder and you will normally be asked a fair price on this basis. This will probably be a minimum of about £20 for a breed in good supply.

The early care and attention and very basic toilet training that your puppy receives is very important for its future development as it is at this age that many bad habits can be formed unless you are gently firm with it. Both the looking after and basic training are not difficult and you should follow the expert advice on this which is given in several of the books I have included in the book list on page 158. These are written by people who know a great deal about bringing up dogs and you will find their advice and guidance very important to you. I would strongly advise you to read one of these before you buy your puppy so that you can plan in more detail for its needs and make a wise buy.

5 Cats

The cat is one of the oldest of our pet animals having been domesticated for over 5000 years. There is a long history and folklore about it which makes very interesting reading. The cat was domesticated from the wild cats of Europe and Asia. The ancient Egyptians kept cats and there are some beautiful sculptures and tomb paintings of them. They were used for hunting and to control vermin. One of their deities, Bast, was portrayed as a cat.

Today cats are probably the most popular of the larger domestic animals as they are comparatively easy to look after and much less demanding than a dog. They are extremely independent creatures and although they are very affectionate it is on their own terms. For some cats their attachment is very much more to their home and where they are looked after than to a particular individual. Others, however, may show a strong attraction for a particular person. Because of this independent nature there is a tendency for some owners to rather neglect their cat, letting it fend for itself rather too much.

Cats are relatively long lived if properly cared for but their way of life makes them prone to accidents, especially on the roads. Because of their attachment to a particular place it is best to start with a kitten rather than a grown cat. However, many people start off looking after a stray cat that frequents the area and which then decides to move in.

Quite a lot of people are allergic to cats and the presence of a cat in a room or even elsewhere in the house may be enough to start an attack of hay fever, asthma or allergic skin reactions of varying severity. This allergy may already be present in a person but it can also develop gradually over the years. Before choosing a cat as a pet do make sure your family is not allergic to them and watch out for symptoms of an allergy developing.

There are a number of varieties of cat all of which have their particular points of interest and attraction. Most are of the British kind and include both long and short-haired varieties and many different colours and markings. Of the foreign types the best known are the Siamese, Abyssinian and Russian Blue. Distinctive varieties are produced by breeders and the more exotic ones can fetch a lot of money especially if they are bred from prizewinners. Cats are naturally prolific breeders and a great many kittens are the result of unplanned matings so that there is invariably someone local looking for homes for kittens. In practice, this is how most kittens are obtained. I do not believe in supporting indiscriminate breeding, though often a young queen (female cat) is mated by a stray tom without the owner realising it. Another ready source of kittens is via your local veterinary surgeon who is often asked by his clients to find homes for kittens that would otherwise be put down. As with any young animal, when you take it from its litter and the surroundings that it has known all its life, a kitten will be upset and frightened. It is up to you and your family to help to make it feel at home by providing sympathetic care and attention to help it adjust to its new surroundings and companions. Warmth and comfort are essential, along with companionship. This does not, however, mean pursuing a kitten around the house to pick it up and cuddle it every few minutes. The kitten is likely to be terrified by such behaviour as it may well not have been handled much before. Be patient and be gentle with your kitten and let it take the initiative towards friendship once it has settled into its surroundings. In this way you will rapidly gain its confidence. It is because of the considerable emotional needs and problems of all young animals that the very worst time to acquire one is at Christmas when there are so many other problems to cope

How to pick up a cat

with at home. Do wait until Christmas or other very busy times are passed so that your young pet can receive the sympathetic care and attention it needs in adjusting to its new home.

Cats are undemanding in their accommodation as they will invariably be kept in the house and take free run of it whether you like it or not. The main indoor requirement is a comfortable sheltered bed where the cat can sleep both during the day and night without constant interruption or disturbance. Cats do not like being disturbed when they are asleep and can become very upset and irritable if this happens too often. There is a good chance that if your choice of bed is not to its liking your cat will choose one that it prefers and as long as the choice is not too inconvenient or unsuitable you will do well to accept its decision.

68

Cats in the wild are basically nocturnal animals, that is they are active mostly at night. This is the time in their natural habitat when they would do most of their hunting, with perhaps another activity period during the daytime. This nocturnal pattern has been partly suppressed in domestication and also by habituation to the routine of the household in which the cat lives, but the basic instinct is still very much there. This does not mean, as some cat owners seem to think, that they should put their cat out of doors to roam at night and then let it in again when they get up in the morning. The cat will have spent a miserable night, may well have got hurt or caught a chill, and will have spent most of the night wanting to be back warm and dry in its bed. Some exercise in the evening will be appreciated but the cat should be able to spend the night in its bed. It is possible to fit a hinged flap into a door so that the cat can come and go as it pleases. If you live near a busy road it is as well to shut your cat in at night. Cats roam over a considerable area even when they are living with a family. There are also, in both towns and the countryside, many domestic cats living wild. These feral cats can be a considerable nuisance causing disturbance during the night, catching and killing other livestock, and spreading disease and parasites. In the countryside many gamekeepers would consider domestic and feral cats the main predator on their birds. It is a feature of cats as pets that the owner gets most of the pleasure and someone else the problems, such are the habits of cats!

An adult cat will require two meals a day, usually given in the morning and evening. One meal is normally of meat, the other of meal or biscuit soaked in milk. Cats should normally be fed meat either raw or cooked. Occasional cooked fish can also be given but too much fish will often cause an allergic skin condition. Cats also require roughage and ideally this should be given in the form of vegetables incorporated in the main feed, but if lacking cats will normally eat coarse fresh grass instead. Where a cat has to be kept indoors the grass should be grown from seed in trays so that a fresh supply is always available.

Some of the things you need for a cat

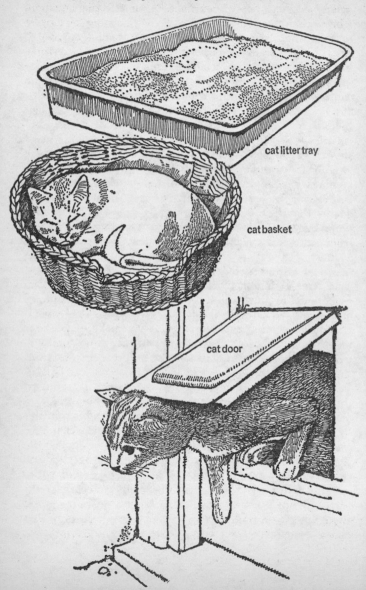

cat litter tray

cat basket

cat door

Whenever possible it is better if you can prepare your cat's food fresh, but for many people it is far easier and more convenient to feed a proprietary brand of tinned food. Most of these tinned foods are complete ones, being a mixture of meat, cereal, bone, added vitamins, oils etc., and some include fish or are based substantially on fish. These complete foods can be given for both meals together with some milk. In addition to milk it is essential that the cat is given fresh water at all times. Milk should be treated as a food and not as a thirst quencher. Cats can be very choosy feeders and this can make it difficult to vary their food. A cat accustomed to freshly prepared food each day will generally accept quite readily the necessary variations and additions to this. When using proprietary brands it is a good idea to use several varieties indiscriminately to avoid habituation to a particular make. Manufacturers recommend about one and a half small tins per cat a day as a general guide to feeding. It is more difficult to calculate the amount of freshly prepared food but a basic 110–140g (4–5 oz) of meat with added vegetable and cereal should be tried, together with milk and a few drops of cod liver oil or similar fish oil. The cost of feeding tinned food and milk is between 25p and 35p per day (June 1978 figures) depending on the brand chosen and where it is purchased.

Cats have very small stomachs and do not require a large meal, hence the twice daily feeding regime compared with the single feed in dogs. Cats are very fastidious in their feeding habits and will not eat food that is stale or contaminated or fed in dirty vessels. When fed the food should be finished up within a few minutes, and if the cat leaves its meal after eating some the food should be taken away and no more given until the next meal. Feeding dishes should be washed after each meal. By observation you should be able to judge the amount of food your cat prefers at a meal and by watching its weight as well you will be able to judge the amount actually required. If the cat is off its food watch out for any signs of illness and if the lack of appetite persists for any length of time, or other symptoms develop, contact your vet. You may suspect that your cat is getting fed elsewhere, especially if the apparent lack of appetite persists without other symptoms. Do, however, check that the utensils are thoroughly clean and that the food offered is fresh. Failing this try some other brands of food, the cat may simply have taken a dislike to a particular one. This is not uncommon because the ingredients do vary considerably between them.

If your cat is pregnant, especially towards the end of pregnancy and when nursing the number of meals should be increased to three or four per day and additional milk and fish oil should be given. Kittens are normally weaned at about six weeks of age but from about three to four weeks they should be given milk to supplement the mother's milk. During the seventh week the weaned kitten can be fed on milk to which is gradually introduced some cereal and finely minced or scraped meat. The weaned kittens should be fed whenever they call for food in the first few weeks but thereafter they should be introduced and kept to a regular routine of four feeds per day up until they are about four months old. Over this period the food given should be progressively firmed up towards the pattern of the adult meal. Between four and six months the kittens should be on to the adult menu and be progressively adjusted to only two feeds per day.

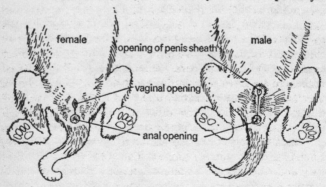

Although the sex of kittens can usually be told at birth, it can be established with more certainty when they are about a week old

Cats are normally able to keep themselves and their coats thoroughly clean and in tip-top condition. Cats should not be bathed and any coat problems involving cleaning should be done using a dry shampoo. Parasites in the coat, particularly fleas, are dealt with by dusting with a specific powder, and at the same time the cat's bedding should also be treated. Long-haired cats will need to have their coats brushed and combed to help them keep clean. All cats swallow a certain amount of hair when grooming, and especially with long-haired varieties it is customary to give them liquid paraffin once a week which as a gentle laxative helps them to pass the hair in their faeces. This might otherwise accumulate as balls of hair in the stomach. Problems don't often arise with the smooth-haired varieties but the routine is certainly to be recommended for the fluffy, long-haired animals.

Cats generally remain quite fit and healthy and any injury or off-colour condition is usually spotted quite readily. They can be very quarrelsome, and any cuts and scratches which result from fighting should be bathed in salt and water and then dusted with an antibiotic powder to prevent infection. More substantial cuts may require to be stitched by a veterinary surgeon. Routine checking should be carried out to see that all is well with the claws and also that the ears and skin are free of parasites. A first sign of something wrong is the scratching or pawing of the area. Ears are very delicate things and occasionally irritation is caused by a foreign body such as a seed lodged there. Occasionally it will be noticed that there are tiny crusts in the ear indicating canker, which is caused by a tiny parasitic mite. This can be alleviated by gentle cleaning with warm olive oil over a period, though further treatment may be necessary to clear it up completely.

Cats are especially susceptible to two killer diseases, infectious feline enteritis and cat 'flu, sometimes referred to as feline distemper. Feline enteritis is a disease which is always about because of the large numbers of stray and unprotected cats. Kittens can be inoculated against this from the age of seven weeks either by one or two injections depending on the system favoured by your veterinary surgeon.

Subsequently booster injections can be given to maintain protection. There is no vaccine available for cat influenza, it is a serious disease and in most cases is fatal if left untreated. It can, however, be cured if treatment is given when the first symptoms of sneezing appear. Both of these diseases are highly infectious and it is quite possible for you or a visitor to spread the virus from one cat to another. It is very important that, as with puppies, you keep any kittens away from possible contacts before the inoculation can be given and become effective. If you suspect that your cat has one of these conditions or requires treatment before inoculation is effective do not take it to the surgery but telephone your veterinary surgeon first for advice.

Like dogs, cats carry both tapeworms and roundworms in their digestive tract. Roundworms, which resemble small, thin, pink earthworms (but are quite unrelated) may be seen in the kitten's motions or occasionally be vomited. Young animals are normally treated routinely for these worms as almost every animal has them and infection has nothing to do with how you look after your cat, or your home. Treatment is simple and has no side-effects. It consists of medication given in the form of a tablet or powder, the dose being according to age and weight. Tapeworms are detected by noting the segments of the worm passed in the faeces. They look like grains of rice, are white in colour and are generally wriggling. Tapeworms are caught in most cases by the animal having swallowed an infected flea, so that it is usual to de-flea the animal and its bedding at the same time as an oral dose is administered to deal with the tapeworm. It is a good idea to have a regular programme of dosing and treatments as frequently the cat is affected without showing any obvious symptoms. It is generally said that a female cat is able to breed for the first time when about nine months old or that it will not come into breeding condition until spring. This is not always the case as many owners know to their considerable embarrassment. To be on the safe side you would be advised to consider any female cat over five months of age as potentially able to breed. Cats are prolific breeders.

Genuine wildcats may produce one or occasionally two litters of two to three kittens each per year, of which only a few would reach maturity. The domesticated cat can easily produce three litters, often of four to six or even more young, during the year most of which will survive. If your cat is accidently mated then your veterinary surgeon can give an injection to prevent the pregnancy if this is done very soon afterwards.

Breeding is a very real problem for cat owners. Unfortunately because there are so many stray male cats roaming about it is almost a certainty that any female cat coming into season is going to be mated. Adult male cats, referred to as toms – the females are called queens – do not make good pets. They are big and strong, independent, often bad-tempered and regularly go missing. They smell very strongly and mark their territory with an equally strongly-smelling secretion, and also with urine. They fight with other cats, especially toms, and regularly need running repairs. Because of this it is usual for any male kittens that are going to be kept as pets to be castrated when they are between four and five months of age.

This operation, often called neutering, is simple and has no unpleasant side effects. The neutered male makes an ideal pet cat. Because it is so difficult to prevent a female from becoming pregnant very careful management is necessary if pregnancy is to be avoided. If you do not want to breed from your cat then it is advisable to have her neutered also. The operation will be done by your vet. All sort of things are said about the nature of neutered cats most of which are quite incorrect. They make ideal pets and do not become overfat or inactive unless they are being overfed. A neutered animal requires less food than an intact one.

If the queen is to be kept intact and allowed to breed she should be restricted to one or at most two litters during the year. The duration of pregnancy is about eight weeks and the young, which are born with their eyes closed, will not leave the nest until they are about four weeks of age and as we have seen, will be weaned at about six weeks. A few days before the birth is due the queen will look out for a suitable quiet, and often darkened, place in which to give birth, and this should be provided with newspaper and cloth so that she can arrange these materials to make a suitable nest. It is possible that the queen may decide not to have her kittens in the house and I have known a house cat choose an underground den in an adjoining plantation in which to have and rear her young. Generally the queen will be able to manage the births herself and she should not be interfered with or disturbed during the process unless in difficulty. If you intend to breed cats or think you may wish to you will need to read and find out more about them. In any case there are a great many books about cats that you will find interesting to read.

6 Rabbits

The original home of the rabbit is southern Europe but they are now found living wild in most European countries, having been spread there by man. They have also been introduced to many other countries. In the past rabbit meat and fur has been greatly valued and it was for these purposes that the rabbit was introduced to Britain in medieval times. They were kept in very large enclosures with artificial mounds of earth in which to dig their burrows. Rabbits were then known as coneys and the name survives in some areas as 'coney banks', a descriptive name for these former rabbit farms, the correct term for which is warrens. Rights of warren – that is the right to keep rabbits or to manage an existing colony – were very valuable and the people who controlled them were known as warreners. These warrens were very well organised and often covered hundreds of acres! In the nineteenth century many warrens fell into disrepair and the rabbits colonised the surrounding countryside and began to eat the farmers' crops. Rabbit trapping was carried out on a considerable scale both to protect the crops and to provide meat for sale. Wild rabbits are excellent to eat but the market for them collapsed in the 1950s when the myxomatosis virus was introduced from Australia into the wild rabbit population. The disease is spread by the rabbit flea and it has greatly reduced the rabbit population, having a mortality rate of about 90 per cent.

Rabbits have for many years been kept and bred for meat, and many of the larger breeds such as the Flemish Giant were developed to be intensively reared for the table.

Rabbits have, however, always been prized as pets and there are a great many attractive varieties which make excellent pets for children. They are straightforward to care for and very rewarding to keep. Rabbits can be kept either out of doors or indoors in a light, well ventilated shed. It is however, very important to choose the right kind of rabbit and to get it from a correct source according to whether it will be kept indoors or out. It is preferable if for most of the year the rabbit is kept outside. They are well able to stand up to the cold if properly housed but this must also give adequate protection against damp and draughts which are particularly harmful to them. If they are to be kept outside do get your stock from someone who keeps them outside as well so that they are accustomed to it. Do not get your rabbit from, say, a laboratory breeding stock that is accustomed to being kept in a warm room in a very small cage and then put it outside. It will almost certainly take a chill. Further, many of the laboratory strains would not stand up to outside conditions as their coats are often very thin.

There are many different varieties of rabbit to choose from. The largest are the Flemish Giants which grow to about 5kg (11 lb) and are really quite unsuitable as pets. The smallest are probably the Polish and Dutch Dwarf varieties which weigh about 1.3kg (3 lb) as adults. There are many varieties in between these sizes. Rabbits can be very strong and difficult for a child to handle if not well tamed and handled so I would suggest starting with one of the smaller breeds. It is a good idea to visit some local shows where rabbit classes are held to get an idea of the different breeds being kept and what they are like. This should also enable you to contact the local rabbit society whose members are probably the best source of stock once you have made up your mind about the kind you would like. Pet shops don't very often keep any pure strains and often only have the unwanted youngsters from a local commercial breeder. You may, however, find that rabbit fanciers advertise young stock there. It will depend very much whereabouts in the country you live just how much choice will be available locally, as interest in rabbit keeping and showing is stronger in some places than others. Another source of stock is through the advertisement column of *Cage and Aviary Bird* or *Fur and Feather* magazines. Much work goes into producing a good litter of rabbits and you could pay quite a lot of money for a really good quality animal from a leading breeder. However, your rabbit need not cost you more than a few pounds and if you are buying from a local enthusiast and are really interested in rabbit keeping you may find you get started for very little.

There are several ways of keeping rabbits; in a hutch with an outdoor run or in a large outdoor enclosure. Keeping rabbits in small hutches is not very attractive for a life-long pet and is a method used mainly when rearing for meat. Large outdoor enclosures are for the more advanced keeper or zoo and I shall therefore only talk about keeping rabbits in a hutch and run system which is much the most pleasant way for all concerned.

One thing is almost certain, you will have to make the hutch and run for yourself, or get your father to do it, as although a few pet shops sell what they optimistically call rabbit hutches I have yet to see one that could be described as adequate. Many of those sold as rabbit hutches are only big enough for one guinea pig. Equally, few of them would stand up to outdoor conditions. Better hutches and sheds can be obtained from specialist suppliers but are quite costly. Hutches are easy to make and are quite inexpensive. For a medium size rabbit the *minimum* dimensions of a hutch would be 120cm (4 ft) long by 60cm (2 ft) deep by 60cm (2 ft) high. This includes a partitioned-off end as a sleeping compartment. If more than one rabbit is to be kept at least another 60cm (2 ft) should be added to the length. The hutch should be solid on three sides including over the nest box, the front being a wooden frame covered in 26mm (1 in) mesh and hinged downwards to facilitate cleaning. The roof should also be hinged and should be sloped and have a considerable overhang all round to provide protection from the weather and let the rain run off. It should be waterproofed by covering it either with several layers of thick polythene or roofing felt.

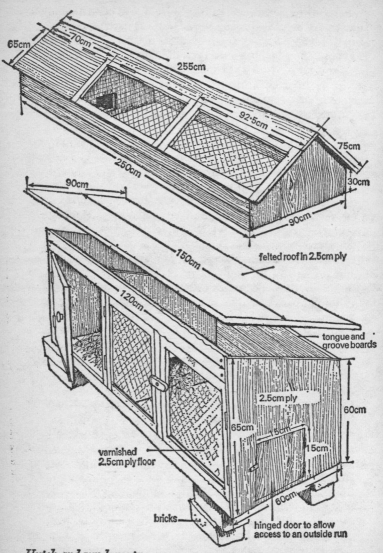

65cm

70cm

255cm

92·5cm

75cm

250cm

30cm

90cm

90cm

150cm

felted roof in 2.5cm ply

120cm

tongue and
groove boards

2.5cm ply

65cm

5cm

15cm

60cm

varnished
2.5cm ply floor

bricks

60cm

hinged door to allow
access to an outside run

*Hutch and run layouts
suitable for both rabbits and guinea pigs*

The hutch floor should be solid, and it is a good idea to protect it with polyurethane varnish. This prevents it becoming impregnated with urine and enables the wood to be cleaned and disinfected more thoroughly. The hutch should not be placed on the ground, but raised either on bricks or on legs. A sliding door can be provided which gives free access to the pen from one end but which can be closed to shut the rabbits in at night, or in very bad weather. It is damp, not cold, that is the problem. The hutch should be provided with a layer of sawdust and straw should be available for bedding. Alternatively newspaper torn up or shredded will make a very good bedding and cage lining. Soiled paper and sawdust should be removed daily.

The outdoor hutch and run will be satisfactory for most of the year and your rabbit accustomed to living outside will have no problem in coping with much of the winter, including snow. However, parts of winter, especially in some areas of the country, can be very wet and nasty and then it is a good idea if the hutch can be brought into a cool shed, garage or outhouse for a couple of months or just while the bad weather lasts. On fine days the hutch can be put outside again for a few hours.

Rabbits feed mainly on green plants, cereals and root crops. In captivity it is usual to feed them twice a day and they will, of course, also be able to graze in the outside run. Rabbits take a wide variety of succulent pasture and hedge-row plants as well as shoots, buds and the leaves of bushes. The green food should be supplemented by some roots and especially by cereals such as stale bread, oats and a little bran. It is very important not to give rabbits too much of any one kind of plant, especially cabbages and clovers. It is also essential to avoid frost damaged or spoiled greens and roots which can cause severe digestive upset. A daily mixture of some cereal plus greens and roots in season will keep your rabbit fit and well. In winter and for breeding does a hot mash of oats and bran with some boiled potatoes, vegetables and scraps will be much appreciated. Rabbits can also be fed on commercial rabbit pellets which are a complete food in a convenient form to store and dispense. It is a good idea, especially in winter when fresh food in any variety is in short supply, to include a proportion of pellets in the daily menu. Food should be supplied in dishes and cut greens or hay should be hung clear of the ground so that they are not spoiled by trampling.

If you wish to breed rabbits it is best to take your doe to a buck to be mated. Does should not be mated until they are at least six months old. Does come into season quite regularly and you can tell by the way her genital area swells that she is ready to be mated. The doe is put in with the buck and if she is ready will normally be mated in a few minutes, that is all that is usually necessary. The young take approximately thirty-one days to develop and when born are blind and naked. The doe will require a dark chamber in which to have the young and will build a nest from hay or straw and line it with fur from her breast. She may begin making this nest as much as two weeks ahead. As her time approaches she should not be disturbed and handled but left in peace and quiet apart from the regular feeding routine. She should not be disturbed for several days after the birth as otherwise she may well destroy the whole litter. It is also essential at this time to make certain that she has a large supply of fresh water, as thirst is another major reason for her eating the young. By about five days the young will be covered in fur and by ten or eleven days their eyes are usually open. At about three weeks they will begin to leave the nest and to nibble the food supplied for the mother. They can be left with the mother till about seven weeks before being weaned from her. At about three months the males and females must be separated. In order to get the youngsters tame they should be handled and gentled as soon as they begin to leave the nest.

It is occasionally said that rabbits should be handled by their ears. How would you like to be picked up by your ears? This is utterly wrong and to do so would cause great pain and damage. The correct way to pick up a rabbit is with a hand underneath the hindquarters to take the weight and a steadying hand over the head. If the rabbit has to be held, as for

How to handle a rabbit

examination, it should be grasped by the loose skin at the back of the neck with the other hand again supporting the weight under the hindquarters.

There are no inoculations for rabbits and kept as described they should be very healthy. There are, however, certain conditions to watch out for. A bloated stomach caused by too much greenstuff can be treated by administering a little bicarbonate of soda in warm milk and supplying only dry food and hay. If it persists telephone your vet for advice. In hot weather it is possible for your rabbit to suffer from sunstroke so do ensure that shade is always available. Cut out any hot mashes and reduce cereals during the summer. The most serious condition a rabbit can develop is coccidosis, when your pet will really look unwell and will have diarrhoea. The skin below the fur will often look yellowish. This can be treated with an antibiotic obtainable from your vet. You may also find that your pellet food incorporates a small dose of antibiotic specifically to prevent the appearance of the disease.

As with other pets you will need to periodically check the coat, ears, and claws to see that all is well. Ear mites can cause canker in the ear and this can be treated as for cats (see page 73). It is also possible that your rabbit may pick up fleas and its coat should be periodically dusted as a preventive measure. This is important because it is the rabbit flea that transmits the myxomatosis virus. Your rabbit could easily catch this disease from a wild rabbit. It is highly infectious, so never pick up a wild rabbit and introduce it into your enclosure without first quarantining it for a month well away from your pets to make sure that it is not incubating the disease. Deflea it immediately on arrival.

Rabbits are relatively inexpensive to keep as much of their food can be gathered for free. I would think that you should be able to feed your rabbit for under 10p a day in winter, which is the most expensive time.

7 Guinea pigs or cavies

One of the most attractive and suitable animals as a children's pet is the guinea pig, or cavie as it is also known. Guinea pigs are not pigs nor do they come from Guinea. They are in fact middle-sized rodents about as big as a young rabbit. Their original home is Peru, where they were kept as pets by the Incas. They were brought to Europe during the seventeenth century mainly by the Spanish and later were distributed around other countries and subsequently all over the world. They have become very popular as pets but are also well known as one of the first laboratory test animals. Hundreds of thousands of them are used the world over for all kinds of statutory testing of drugs, medicines, cosmetics and so on. They are the origin of the expression 'to be used as a guinea pig', meaning to be used to try out something.

Guinea pigs come in three distinct coat varieties, namely smooth-haired, long-haired Peruvians, and Abyssinian rosettes in which the hair is arranged in tufted whorls. In each of these varieties there are many different colours ranging from albino white through grey to black, and with a rich variety of sandy and chestnut colours. The plain coloured ones are said to be self-coloured whilst those with patches of different colours are simply referred to as coloured. These coloured ones are particularly attractive, with a tremendous variety and pattern of markings.

Both the smooth-coated and the Abyssinian are not difficult to keep, though our own experience has been that the Abyssinian is perhaps not quite as hardy as the smooth-coated ones, and is more prone to illness, though this could be due to the particular stock which we were given. The Peruvian is a silky, long-haired variety that has been produced by breeders for its interest and appeal. You do not get them in the wild. They are not very often seen and I would not recommend them unless you have already become a guinea pig fanatic. Their coats are very long and silky and need constant attention. In addition to that they are not very hardy. You certainly couldn't keep them outside.

Guinea pigs if well looked after should live to about five years. Some can live a few years longer, but many kept as pets average about two to three years, often succumbing to a chill or infection from other stock. You may be able to obtain guinea pigs from a friend or equally from a local breeder or fancier. Look out for adverts or consult the specialist papers, and do go along to local shows to see what kinds are available locally. I do not advise buying or being given an adult from a laboratory stock. These are almost always albinos and my reason for this caution is that unless they have been handled and petted, which is very unlikely, laboratory stocks are invariably very timid and frightened. They have spent most of their life in a very small bare cage with almost no contact with other guinea pigs or humans and therefore they are very unhappy at the change to new accommodation and to the increased contact with people. It can take several years for an adult to fully adjust to the change. I would advise buying a pair – probably a litter pair of the same sex – when they are still quite young, say about four weeks old. They can grow up together in the new surroundings. Later on you may be encouraged to run a small colony of guinea pigs, which can be great fun. Guinea pigs, especially those of good quality, are not all that easily obtained. Most pet shops seem only to have a few from time to time and these often leave much to be desired. It will certainly pay you to look around for a bit to find a source of good, healthy, friendly stock. You should be prepared to pay several pounds for the right kind of animal and a really good one will cost you quite a lot of money.

Guinea pigs can be kept in hutches very similar to those that I have described for rabbits on page 79. The minimum size for a hutch is about 105 × 60 × 60 cm (3 ft 6 in × 2 ft × 2 ft) but for most of the year a system of an outdoor hutch with a sliding door leading into an outdoor enclosure is preferred. This can be a permanent site, but it is preferable if the animals can be moved around to fresh ground every few days. That way you get your grass mown and fertilised. Guinea pigs are quite playful and they will enjoy 'toys' such as drainpipes and branches placed in their outdoor run. Once autumn begins it is advisable to bring the hutch indoors into a garage or shed and only put it out during the day when it is fine. Damp and wind are the most unpleasant conditions for animals rather than cold alone. Guinea pigs are not as hardy as rabbits. In some parts of the country it is possible to keep a hutch outside for the winter if double-walled sleeping boxes and plenty of straw or newspaper are provided, and the hutch can be sited in a sheltered position. Another way in which guinea pigs can be kept indoors, say in a light and airy shed or garage, is by enclosing part of the floor. Wooden planking about 30cm (12 in) high or even a wall of loose bricks can be used to make the enclosure. Sleeping boxes are provided according to the numbers being kept, and these stand free within the enclosure. Most of the floor should be covered with straw, and fresh straw added daily and the badly soiled straw removed. This is called a deep litter system, and both guinea pigs and rabbits do very well on it. The deeper layers of the straw ferment producing heat, thus contributing to the warmth and comfort of the animals. The deep litter, which by then is good manure below, is usually cleared at the end of the winter. If a concrete floor is being used as the base it is advisable to leave a part of this uncovered as its rough surface will help to keep the claws worn down, otherwise these will have to be trimmed from time to time.

Guinea pigs are plant feeders but it is very important to realise that they cannot live on grass and greens alone. They have prodigious appetites and when out at grass will eat for most of the day. They are also notorious for eating up their meals very quickly so that someone may often get shouted at for not having fed their pets! They have comparatively small

long-haired Peruvian

Abyssinian rosette

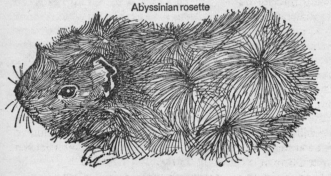

smooth-haired

Varieties of guinea pig

stomachs so they need to be fed or to have access to food in reasonable amounts for most of the time. The food should consist of a mixture of things such as fresh greens (say cabbage, lettuce, hedgerow plants, leaves and freshly cut grass), root crops (such as carrots, turnips and swedes) and a cereal (such as bread, bruised oats and flake maize). These foods can usefully be supplemented with a few commercial rabbit pellets. In the summer grass can form the bulk of the green food with a taste of any others available, plus root crops in season. At all times there should be dry cereal or pellet food available plus some hay. In winter cabbage is likely to be the main source of greenstuff and at this time root crops, which are then in season, and the cereal and pellet foods can be increased. We have found it satisfactory to provide additional food in the morning and evening leaving the natural foods and cereals available through the day. The quantities fed will have to be judged on the condition of your animals, but don't let them get too fat. Guinea pigs will try and fatten themselves for the winter and if this has happened their food during the winter should be reduced to ensure that they use up their fat. This can only be done by reducing the total intake of food and not by leaving them unfed or by cutting out meals. That is the surest way to make them very ill. In the winter a guinea pig will appreciate a hot meal once a day and this should be given at night. It can comprise bran and cereals with cooked potato, brown bread, milk and so on.

Guinea pigs fed on a soft diet, which for practical purposes means most pet ones, may develop trouble with their front incisor teeth. These teeth work like a pair of chisels nipping off grass, twigs, etc., and the wear this produces keeps pace with their slow growth. If the food is too soft the teeth do not wear as fast as they grow and they may become overgrown, which results in considerable difficulty in eating and possibly pain and discomfort. It is advisable to provide all rodents with something they can gnaw at to keep the teeth in good condition. Probably the most attractive is a piece of fresh branch. Many animals find the bark and the layers immediately below it particularly appetising.

Guinea pigs like branches of wood to gnaw

As with all animals it is very important not to vary the diet too rapidly and to avoid too much clover, cabbage or lettuce at any one time. Make any changes in the diet gradually. Never feed frost damaged, bad or bruised greens, fruits or vegetables. Trim off any damaged or spoiled area before feeding. Your guinea pig requires access to clean water at all times and when feeding on dry foods will require very much more than when eating moist foods. If you are using water bottles – which is the most satisfactory method – you should have the large 500 cc bottle, which should be filled twice daily for two guinea pigs. Guinea pigs are very economical animals to feed and the cost during the winter should not be more than 50p a week, and could be less.

As long as there is sufficient room guinea pigs will usually live amicably together and breeding poses no special problems. Guinea pigs can produce two to three litters a year and the number of young in a litter is normally up to four. Female guinea pigs should be at least six months old before they are allowed to breed and they may need to run with the male for several weeks before they become pregnant. It is advisable, if you intend to breed with your stock, to get a suitable male of your own. Failing this it may be possible to borrow a male or let your females visit one. There is, however, always the risk of them picking up an infection and for this reason I prefer to keep our stock self contained. The male can be left to run with the females and the young as long as they get on well together, which is usually the case.

It is very difficult to predict when the young will be born because it may be several weeks before the pair mate and they are very discreet about mating, in contrast to rabbits. The gestation period is about seventy days although long before this the females begin to look very obviously pregnant and thereafter seem to go on and on until you think they might burst! Pregnant females are very delicate and you should avoid picking up and handling them unless it is absolutely necessary to do so. If you are running a colony make sure that there are some spare nest boxes and fresh bedding available so that the mother has a choice of where to give birth. If you are keeping a pair in a hutch a separate extra nest chamber should be provided or the mother separated into a separate hutch on her own as the time gets nearer or when she shows signs of feeling her pregnancy. The mother should be left to give birth unaided; there are things that can go wrong with the delivery of the litter, or just with a particular baby, but there is nothing that you can do to help in the normal course of things and the mother is best able to cope with them herself. The delivery of the litter will normally take a couple of hours but if she shows signs of trouble or discomfort much after this you should telephone your vet for advice. The most common problem is a mis-presentation of the youngster, with it being delivered backside first rather than head first. This causes difficulty in delivery. The delay is usually fatal for the baby concerned and can sometimes affect the rest of the litter. Young guinea pigs are fully developed at birth though the mother has to wash and clean them and she should not be disturbed whilst she is doing this. The young are born one at a time and some cleaning of the young is usually done before the delivery of the next. After the young have been born the mother will deliver pieces of the placenta which should be removed. There can be a considerable difference in the size of the youngsters which is due to their position within the uterus and the relative amount of food each was able to obtain via the placenta. The young guinea pigs will be weaned in about two to three weeks and it is advisable when they are about three months of age to remove any young females for several months until they are fully grown and can be safely bred from. During pregnancy the mother should have plenty of food in good variety and will also benefit from being given oil, milk and extra vitamins, particularly those contained in the liver oils. Extra feeding should be maintained during lactation and the milk should be continued as there is an especially heavy demand on the mother for calcium, phosphorus and other minerals present in milk. From a few days of age the young will begin to eat a little of the food provided for the adults and they too can be given extra milk. Do make sure that there is plenty of water available for the mother. It is also a good idea to add a small, low, water bottle that the babies can reach.

For general health precautions those described for the rabbit, namely routine examination of the coat for parasites, the ears, teeth and claws are all that is normally required. Digestive upsets are usually due to similar causes as those of the rabbit and should be treated likewise. Generally speaking you will find guinea pigs to be very fit and healthy animals that should give you few problems.

8 Mice

For many years a mouse was one of the most popular of children's pets though today they are less frequently kept in some parts of the country than others. There is, however, a very strong following amongst both children and adults for all manner of fancy mice, particularly in the Midlands and the North. The present-day fancy mouse is ultimately descended from the domestic house mouse. Not surprisingly there maybe parental prejudice against keeping mice in some quarters, but they really are attractive, interesting, friendly, little animals that soon overcome prejudices once you get started – always the first hurdle!

Mice come in a great many different colour varieties from the great range of self-colours from white through reds and yellows to black, and a similar variety of colours, markings and patterns in the so-called marked mice. Most mice are smooth coated but a number of varieties of coat have been produced.

Mice are highly social, quite gregarious animals, although their social structure within the colony is very complex and highly organised. The big question always to be faced with mice is whether to keep just one or to have a small colony which means that they will breed regularly. A small colony is so interesting and fascinating that I would advise anyone starting to go for this in a small way and to face up to the problem of having to dispose of the surplus youngsters. Whatever you do, do not start with a large number of mice. One male and perhaps two females is quite enough to begin with as within the month you could easily find that they have produced sixteen or more babies! As with many of these fancied pets I would advise you to have a good look at the many different varieties being kept and shown and on offer for sale. To get any of the more unusual varieties you will almost certainly have to buy from specialist breeders or fanciers, as most pet shops often only have the white ones which are widely kept in laboratories for experimental work.

You will probably be able to obtain your stock quite cheaply for a pound or two each for the more interesting varieties. Do be careful about how you choose your pet. Mice are not dirty, very smelly animals nor do they like to be over-crowded. Beware of stock kept like that. The mice should not be frightened but be friendly and inquisitive. The breeder should be able to pick them up gently by the base of the tail and have them sit quietly on his hand. A certain allowance in this respect has to be made for the very young ones, but do be careful of stock that is difficult to handle and frightened as it means that they have not been well handled from very young, which is important for a pet. Mice are able to breed when they are about eight weeks old but should not be allowed to do so until they are about three months. If you buy young stock then you will need to keep the male separate from the females until they are old enough to breed safely.

Mice manage to live in a great variety of conditions and in small cages. They are, however, creatures that do appreciate space and variety in their home environment and they also naturally exercise quite a lot. Pet shops sell small metal cages fitted with exercise wheels for mice, gerbils and hamsters but they are very much on the small side and are rather cold. One of the most suitable homes for mice and also for hamsters and gerbils is a glass aquarium fitted with a wire mesh lid. This lid is vital for ventilation and you should not use glass or a solid top. Mice live in both the warm and the cold but the real killer for them is damp of any kind, warm or cold. Both are equal killers in damp conditions which may be very rapidly produced in any closed tank. An ideal tank is about 60cm (2 ft) or more long and about 38cm (1 ft 3 in) high and deep. Into this you can add peat or sawdust, logs, pipe tunnels, ladders, a hanging or stretched rope and an exercise wheel which will provide a stimulating environment for them. The

black and white

white

red and white

brown

Pet mice come in a variety of colours, with many different markings

only thing I would add is that the bigger the tank the better, and the fact that it should not be filled with moist peat or soil because of the damp problem.

Mice will use a variety of bedding materials and in the tank type of set-up hay or newspaper should be provided which the mice will then shred to make their own nests.

Many people will prefer to keep their mice indoors and certainly in winter this may be essential, even during the rest of the year they cannot be kept in the open and would need to be in a shed or conservatory. The great objection to mice is their smell. Mice need not smell to any noticeable extent if you do not keep too many of them in a small cage, clean them out regularly and do not have too many males. It is the adult males that are responsible for much of the smell in a colony and also for much of the aggression so that you will not want to keep more than one adult male in your colony at a time. If you want to keep some extra males then keep them separate from each other or create some smaller sub-colonies. If you manage things sensibly and responsibly then you will not have complaints.

Mice feed on a very wide range of foodstuffs, almost as varied as our own. You can buy complete pellet feeds which do keep them in really tip-top condition, but at no expense to yourself, you should be able to feed them from within the home with just a few additions in the form of seeds such as wheat, barley and maize. Brown and white bread, cake, fruit, cereals, vegetables, bacon rind and a little meat will all be eaten by the mice and you can experiment within the framework of an overall balanced diet just what your mice prefer and need. For feeding they do like to have some food available all the time and it is advisable to feed small quantities twice a day. Do not leave food any longer than this as they do tend to soil it. Experiment with the quantities of the different things to find out how much they need per day and then give this in the twice-daily routine.

To keep your pets tame and friendly they should be handled gently out of their cage each day and you will find that they become very attached to you and responsive to this regular handling and fondling. Do not, however, pick up and over-handle the pregnant females as you can cause severe damage to them. If you have to move a pregnant female see if she will walk on to your hand so that you do not have to grasp her or pick her up whilst she is moved. Failing that she should be grasped gently at the base of the tail and your hand eased below her. Never pick up a mouse by the end of its tail; all handling should be done by grasping the base of the tail firmly and gently with the other hand used for support of the body.

If you keep a male and a female mouse together you must expect to have young within a very short time. I feel it is very worthwhile and extremely fascinating to breed mice, and for children it is quite an outstanding experience and achievement. When I maintained a large breeding colony of mice in a museum in London all our visitors, both adults and children, were absolutely captivated by the mothers and their young

How to pick up a mouse

and completely forgot their prejudices about mice as they watched a row of ten baby mice being suckled. It is, however, quite certain that at the end of the day most of the young that are bred are going to have to be disposed of, and this unfortunately means in practice that most of them are going to have to be put down. This is something that has to be faced from the outset and it is better that you accept it rather than imagine that you will find homes for them. Excess mice should be painlessly put to sleep by your veterinary surgeon, and should not under any circumstances be turned loose to die a lingering, shivering death.

The females should have the male added to their colony when they are about three months old. They will normally mate within five days and the gestation period is between nineteen and twenty-one days. The male can remain with the females for as long as you like but he will mate the females again whilst they are still feeding the young and you could well have another litter before the first is fully weaned. This is a strain on the females and it is better if they are rested between litters, (i.e. remove the male mouse.) The female will make a nest of shredded material in which she will have and rear the young. If you provide newspaper or tissues the female will shred this to make her nest and there is no finer, warmer material for a nest than newspaper, which also has the added advantage that it is surprisingly germ free and does not harbour the tiny mites which are often present on straw and hay. Throughout her pregnancy the female will need to have been carefully fed and it is important that some meat or insect food be included, as if the colony is hungry for animal protein there is a danger that some of the babies may be killed and eaten. Plenty of water is also essential. The young are born tiny and naked, blind and deaf, although they grow very quickly. Do not disturb or handle the young for the first few days as this may lead to the abandonment of the litter or their being attacked. A gentle peep into the nest using a pencil to move a little of the bedding whilst the female is feeding will probably do no harm but do be careful. If she is not pleased with her nest she may make another and will then carry the young in her mouth one at a time to the new site. Occasionally you will find a youngster that has been pushed out of the nest and it can be gently slipped back in. Sometimes, however, youngsters are deliberately evicted and this seems to be because there is something wrong with them which may or may not be apparent to us. Do not be surprised if some of the litter is stillborn, that is, born dead.

The babies develop very fast and they will be weaned at about three weeks of age and by six weeks the sexes must be separated. Handling of the youngsters should begin as soon as they begin to explore from the nest so that they associate scent and handling by humans as part of the world which they are beginning to explore and learn about. At that stage you can begin to think about which animals you will keep and which you will be parting with.

9 Golden hamsters

The hamster is a comparative newcomer to the pet scene but has become very popular as a children's pet. To many people it is for a variety of reasons considered to be more suitable than mice. Almost nothing is known about the golden hamster in the wild. The entire captive population is descended from a female with a litter of twelve young found by an expedition from the Hebrew University in Palestine near Aleppo in Syria in 1931. The family was taken to the University and subsequently bred from. Hamsters are nocturnal animals and this is a characteristic that has remained unchanged with domestication. A pet hamster will sleep for most of the day and usually wake up in early evening and then be active for much of the night. In the wild they would spend the day asleep in their burrows protected from the very hot sun and be active when it is cooler at night. In the wild state in winter, when it can be very cold, they normally hibernate in underground burrows, but in captivity if kept in a fairly even temperature they will remain active throughout the year, although some individuals even then will become rather less active than during the rest of the year. As a pet they should not be kept out of doors and even in a good shed the temperature fluctuations will almost certainly be too much for them. You should plan to keep your hamster indoors throughout the year.

Hamsters are very much solitary animals and you cannot keep two adults together as they will almost certainly kill each other. Unless you plan to breed them you will only want to keep one and a young male about six weeks of age is the most suitable to start with. Females are more temperamental than the males. The lifespan is comparatively short, generally less than two years and not more than three to four years. Hamsters still have many of their wild characteristics and are somewhat timid and shy, and will bite if frightened or upset. It is therefore necessary to choose one that shows a good temperament as a youngster and to handle it very gently and carefully to gain its confidence. Provided that this is done your hamster will be a friendly and affectionate pet, but one that should always be treated with respect. If you suddenly grab him or poke your finger into his nest when he is asleep you will fully deserve the sharp, deep bite which you will almost certainly get – it was given in self-defence against an unknown attacker!

Hamsters are active, agile creatures, which is something most people forget unless they have seen one active in a spacious and well-furnished cage. They are not difficult to accommodate but unfortunately will gnaw through almost any form of wooden cage. The metal cages sold for hamsters by most pet stores are much too small and metal is not very good for cages for small mammals because of its coldness and the condensation that forms on it. The most suitable home is probably an aquarium tank made of glass with a wire mesh lid. The latter is essential for proper ventilation. This should be a minimum of about 60 × 30 × 38cm (24 in × 12 in × 15 in) tall. The extra height will allow your pet to climb and makes for a much more interesting environment. The tank should be furnished with a variety of branches and features that will encourage the animal to move around and explore. The branches should be of fresh native hardwood such as oak or beech which your pet will also use to keep his front incisor teeth in good shape. It is not necessary to provide a sleeping compartment as long as a corner of the cage provides a suitable place for a nest to be built. A hamster will chew up all sorts of things with which to make a nest but the most suitable is fine hay or newspaper. Material such as tow is sometimes sold as animal bedding but it is not very suitable as it gets caught in the teeth and claws and if swallowed can cause a blockage of the intestinal tract. Water must always be available and the water bottle with a metal nozzle is to be preferred if your pet does not keep biting through it. If this happens it will be necessary to use a water pot. Hamsters regularly urinate and defecate in the same part of their cage and this habit can be exploited by placing a small toilet tray such as a metal jam pot lid at the chosen spot. Various materials can be used for cage lining including newspaper, sawdust or dry peat, all of which seem to be adequate. Because of their food and their clean toilet habits, a hamster's cage does not need to be cleaned out too frequently and they do not have any noticeable smell. What must be dealt with is the hamster's food hoard, which includes all kinds of food. This is usually formed just behind the bedding and needs to be removed regularly, especially where perishable food is being hoarded.

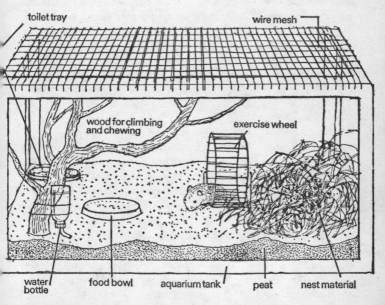

A hamster cage

Hamsters eat a variety of seeds, cereals, fruits and nuts and need only small amounts daily – generally around a heaped tablespoonful will be more than enough. A single daily feed in the evening is all that is required. The menu should be planned so that as far as possible the hamster will be encouraged to eat the perishable food quite soon leaving the non-perishable items to be added to the store. Hamsters nearly always collect their food and then eat it later. In both cheeks they have large pouches which when they find something suitable they will cram full and use to take the food back to the safety of the burrow to eat at leisure. Your hamster may well fret if he is not allowed to do this and you should allow him to accumulate a store. It can be periodically removed and he will simply start another.

A hamster will keep itself well groomed and thoroughly cleaned and the only aid you need give towards this is a balanced diet with the provision of some food rich in oil such as sunflower seeds. These are a very valuable addition to the

A hamster with full (left) and empty (right) pouches

Hamsters groom themselves very carefully. The one on the right is nuzzling its scent gland

basic diets of any seed-eating animal as they supply important oils and proteins in addition to their carbohydrate content. You will almost certainly notice your hamster spending a very great deal of time grooming an area on its side. This is the site of a tiny gland that produces a minute amount of an oily secretion which a hamster spreads throught its fur. It is thought that this is important in the social behaviour of the species and serves as a means of recognising or characterising individuals.

The female hamster can breed from the age of six weeks but should not be mated until she is about three months of age. Males and females are almost totally intolerant of each other except when the female is ready to be mated. The female comes into breeding condition about every three to four days during the summer and this can be recognised by the swelling of the genital area and often by gentle squeaking. The female should always be placed in with the male so that there is less chance of her attacking him. If she is ready to be mated she will be friendly towards him and will soon take up a stiff-legged posture with her tail raised. The male will be keen to mate and several copulations will usually be made in about half an hour. When his or her interest has waned the female should be put back into her cage. If she is initially aggressive towards him, separate them and try again later. The gestation period of the hamster is only sixteen days and the young, like those of mice, are born naked, blind and helpless. During her pregnancy the mother should be given additional food, paying particular attention to balance in the diet, and she should also be offered insects or mealworms together with milk. (Hamsters, like many rodents supposedly vegetarian, often consume some insect or other invertebrate food and if they do not get this may kill and consume some of their young). The female should not be disturbed as her time approaches and the litter should be left at least twenty-four hours before a very careful look is taken, preferably when the mother is occupied feeding. The litter may consist of up to a dozen babies. The eyes open at about fourteen days and at this stage they are quite active, crawling around the nest and outside of it. By about three weeks they will be running about actively. At four weeks or earlier if the mother becomes intolerant of them the young should be removed and the sexes housed separately to prevent premature mating. These can be kept together until they become aggressive to each other (usually when two to three months old) at which stage it means one animal, one cage. When the young are running round the cage they should be accustomed to the human hand and smell and enticed with titbits. When they are weaned they should then be regularly handled and petted.

10 Gerbils

Gerbils are the most recent addition to the group of small mammals kept as pets and have become very popular. Their original home is the arid mountain desert areas of Mongolia and their way of life is very much adapted to desert conditions. Like many desert animals they spend the hotter part of the day in underground burrows and are active above ground in the cooler times and at night. They have large round eyes that are well adapted for seeing in poor light. Despite being partly nocturnal in the wild this is much less marked in captivity than with hamsters.

Another of their adaptations is water conservation and in the wild almost all their water requirement is obtained from green food. This is also the case in captivity though water must always be provided for them. Accommodation similar to that which I described for a hamster is suitable for them but it can be modified to take account of their burrowing instincts. The tank can be about two-thirds filled with a light loamy soil that they can dig tunnels through, some of these will pass close to the glass and you will be able to watch them in the burrows. It is difficult however to maintain the soil at the right consistency for burrowing without the animals becoming damp and chilled. For this reason it is often preferred to construct a series of tunnels by moulding them in plaster of paris or modelling them in wire and coating them with plaster.

Several may live together quite amicably but the normal and the most interesting and satisfactory arrangement is to keep a male and female pair. Gerbils when they pair mostly

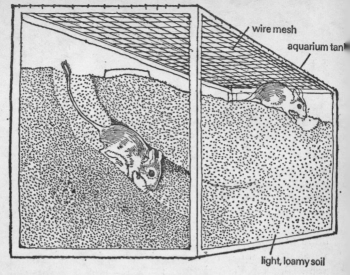

wire mesh

aquarium tank

light, loamy soil

Gerbils should be allowed to burrow in their cage

do so for life and once they have become bonded are unlikely to take to and breed with another. The average lifespan is about two to three years but they can easily live to be four or even five if well cared for.

Gerbils are not difficult to breed from. The pair should be kept together all the time as the male will not attack the young. The gestation period is about twenty-five days and a litter will normally be of about five or six young which are born naked and blind. They grow rapidly and are mature at ten to twelve weeks, though it is advisable to separate the sexes a few weeks earlier to prevent premature breeding.

Gerbils are not difficult to feed and will readily take a mixture of cereals, fruits and vegetables, plus the occasional insect or mealworm.

11 Birds as pets

A great many different kinds of birds are kept and bred in captivity in this country and it is a good thing that in recent years the importation of birds from abroad has been severely restricted so that most foreign birds in this country are now being bred here. It has, however, greatly increased the price of many kinds as it is more expensive to breed them than to import them from the wild thousands of miles away. There are so many different birds available and so much skill and knowledge has been accumulated about their management that if you fancy keeping a particular kind you will need to read up about that species in one of the more specialised books. If you are just beginning to think about keeping pets or about branching out into birds then I would advise you to start with some of the better known kinds such as budgerigars, canaries or zebra finches in order to develop your skill and knowledge through practical experience with them. On the other hand if you have a parent or friend who is knowledgeable about keeping particular kinds or who is keen to expand into other species then by all means do so. Do try and visit other specialist breeders of that species and read up about them in the specialist books and magazine articles.

It is illegal to keep almost all wild British birds in captivity unless these have been bred and ringed in captivity, or the bird has been found in an injured or damaged condition that prevents it from being returned to the wild. I shall talk about keeping such wild birds later on. Pet birds that can be kept outside in our climate with suitable protection and shelter include pigeons, chickens, ducks and geese. Of the foreign

parrot

mynah bird

cockatiel

canary

zebra finch

Some popular cage birds

birds that can be kept out of doors if properly acclimatised and provided with warm indoor accommodation in winter and during bad weather are budgerigars and canaries, many members of the parrot family and various finches, weavers and cardinals. These can also be kept indoors provided suitable accommodation is available. Other species may have to be kept in much more precise conditions and should not be considered unless you are able to provide these conditions and have access to expert help and advice.

Most of the above birds will be kept either in small cages appropriate to the size and type of bird or in a larger indoor or outdoor aviary furnished according to the needs of the birds being kept. A further practice that is likely to develop from one's initial enthusiasm and success is a bird room. This is simply a room in which a variety of cages or aviaries are kept because the collection has outgrown the home! Such a room needs to be planned with care and will require heat and light.

The most practical start to bird keeping is probably to be had from budgerigars or canaries and perhaps chickens or bantams if you have a suitable garden. The budgerigars or canaries can be kept either in an indoor cage or in an outside aviary. The latter is very much more satisfactory and I would urge anyone to consider this method of keeping small birds rather than having just one indoors. Making a start with these simpler species will give a great deal of pleasure and you will gain practical experience of taking care of these birds which is worth a great deal more than reading every book you can about them, though preferably you should do both. None of the equipment which you buy or make for these species will be wasted as it is fairly basic for most of the others which you might wish to go on to. The basic principles described below for keeping budgerigars will give you an indication of the way in which birds need to be looked after. If you would like to keep other kinds of birds read up about them first and find out their special requirements. It is not possible in this book to talk about the needs of all of the many kinds of bird that could be available as a family pet.

Budgerigars

The budgerigar has for many years been the most popular and widely kept of captive birds both as a family pet and by fanciers. It is the smallest of the parrot family and is a native of the wooded and scrub grasslands of Australia where it lives in very large flocks moving around following the supplies of seeds and water. Most of the wild birds are light green in colour but other varieties do appear in the wild flocks from time to time. It is characteristic of budgerigars that they may produce colour varieties quite different from either parent bird and by breeding with these 'sports' or varieties it has become possible to establish many new permanent varieties.

Budgerigars are attractive, friendly, active little birds and make good companions. It is for this reason that many of them are kept singly as indoor pets. It is generally possible to get these individual birds to talk. Kept this way, however, companionship for the bird is important, and they will also need toys and playthings to amuse themselves to make up for the loss of stimulus and contact with their own kind. It is possible to keep two cock birds together and they will become close friends, but if you do this they will not learn to talk. Budgerigars breed readily in captivity and for this reason a male and female pair should not be kept in the usual sort of domestic cage as their breeding activities are invariably frustrated. Under such conditions much of the appeal of the birds is lost because of their concern with breeding and rearing young.

The cages sold by many pet stores for budgerigars are all wire ones, the lower half of which may be enclosed in glass. Often the cages are suspended from a stand. Each cage has a number of perches and is usually fitted with feeding and water hoppers. The floor of the cage consists of a removable tray that can be withdrawn for regular cleaning. These cages are not very satisfactory as they deny the bird many of its basic needs, especially those of security and shelter. They are also rather on the small side for an active bird and in many cases their design and finish is intended to provide an attractive piece of room décor rather than the optimum home for a bird. The principal complaint against these cages is that the bird is vulnerable from all sides and has nowhere to hide or cower if alarmed, and this, in the hustle and bustle of a family household, can be very upsetting and distressing to a young bird. It is also desirable that a part of a cage can be shaded from the light, again to give a more secure feeling, and a bird should also be able to get shade from sunlight or the heat from a fire. Unless fitted with glass sides these cages are also very draughty and subject to great temperature fluctuations. If this type of cage is to be used to accommodate a budgerigar it is important for the welfare of the bird that it should be placed so as to minimise these problems. A corner position, for example, will give protection on two sides.

The more satisfactory type of cage is a simple wooden box with a mesh front. These can be purchased from the better pet shops and specialist suppliers or they can easily be made. The standard-sized cage fronts of wire can be purchased at most stores and fitted to a box of your own construction measuring not less than $60 \times 45 \times 30$cm (2 ft $\times$ 1 ft 6 in $\times$ 1 ft). The box will normally be painted white inside to show off the colour of the birds and it will have a withdrawable metal tray for ease of routine cleaning. The cage should be fitted with a series of perches so that the bird can hop from one to the other. The diameter of the perch should be carefully chosen so that the resting bird is able to grip it easily without developing cramp. Hoppers for both food and water can be attached to the front of the cage.

Budgerigars can be purchased from pet stores and from private breeders and fanciers, and there will almost certainly be a number in your area whose address you will most likely be able to obtain from your pet store or a local society. The price which you pay for your bird will very much depend on its show quality and you will not normally be buying an expensive show winner just as a companion pet. If, however, you are planning an outdoor aviary with a small breeding flock then you will be best advised to get good quality stock.

water hopper

food hopper

The best type of indoor cage for small birds

For pets it is probably better to purchase young male birds but with youngsters it will not be possible to sex them with certainty until after they have moulted, when the cere (the bare patch immediately above the beak) of the male will be blue and that of the female will be brown. The most difficult part of establishing any bird or animal as a pet is that of taming it. You will need a very great deal of patience to get the bird used to your presence and to the activity of the home. You will need to be slow, gentle and patient with it until it has settled down and gained confidence. Never chase your bird around the room trying to catch it, it will be very frightened. If your bird does not return to its cage of its own accord, draw the curtains or darken the room, which will quieten it, and then approach openly, talking to it. Allow it to step on to your finger. I would recommend that you read a book on handling and taming birds because if you start the right way you will have no problems of handling later on. It may well be the sort of thing that as a child you should not do unless you have the patience. Otherwise you should not handle the bird until it is fully trained. Remember that if you do let your bird loose in a room that the doors and windows must be firmly closed, other pets removed, and hazards such as chimneys and open fires guarded.

Budgerigars are very easy to feed in captivity, as in the wild they feed mainly on the seeds of grasses. You will be able to buy a seed mixture for budgerigars from your pet store – normally a mixture of canary seed and millet. This can be supplemented by the occasional few flakes of bruised oats or pin-head oatmeal. The latter is also very useful if you wish to add a drop of linseed feed oil or cod liver oil to the diet, which is very good for their feathers and general well-being. A little drop of the oil is simply allowed to soak into the oats. A number of other seeds can also be added occasionally to provide variety in the diet. Your birds should also be given a little greenstuff regularly, and they will particularly relish spinach, lettuce, dandelion and a number of other garden weeds such as shepherd's purse. In addition it is necessary to supply a calcium-rich grit which should consist of both crushed shell and ground limestone which is necessary for the grinding action of the gizzard and also as the main source of calcium for general health and the production of eggshells. The bird should also have access to a piece of cuttlefish bone.

The most attractive way of keeping budgerigars is in a large outdoor aviary which leads back into a shed housing the roosting quarters, breeding boxes and so on, and which can be heated in winter. This is the arrangement we have here in the part of Scotland where I live because of the uncertainty of the weather. Elsewhere many people would have the nest boxes placed outside. The outside flight should also have solid protection to provide shelter from the wind and from rain in the outside quarters. This is something to be used by the birds if they wish to and will also provide an area of shade wherever the sun happens to be.

Budgerigars will breed very freely in captivity either in a large cage or in the aviary. It is necessary to restrict the breeding of the pair to not more than two or three clutches in a year because of the very considerable strain on the parent birds. In the wild budgerigars nest in hollows in trees and the nest is unlined. In captivity they require a wooden box about 15cm (6in) high, and about 18cm (7 in) wide and long with a hole about 3.8cm (1½ in) in diameter in one side. It is essential that the floor of the nest box should be hollowed so that the clutch of eggs will stay together. No lining material of any kind should be provided. This box can be set up in either the aviary or in the top back corner of the breeding cage which should not measure less than 60 × 45 × 30cm (2ft × 1½ ft × 1 ft) In a breeding colony it will be necessary to provide boxes for each pair of birds which you hope will breed so as to give them a choice of sites. Breeding budgerigars are very aggressive and pugnacious and it would be advisable to provide about three identical boxes per breeding pair in each situation to cope with this problem. In many ways aviary breeding presents a lot of problems and it may well be preferable to withdraw a pair from the aviary into a breeding cage and let them rear young there rather than have the whole colony breeding in an uncontrolled manner.

The breeding season can be started about mid to late February and once the pair have settled in the clutch (usually four to five eggs) should be started after about ten to fourteen days. One egg is laid every two days and unlike most birds incubation begins at once so that the chicks hatch at two-day intervals as well. This is a natural system which tends to regulate the size of the brood according to the supply of food. If there is plenty of food then all the young will be reared but if it is in short supply the older chicks are fed preferentially so that at least a part of the clutch is reared. The breeding birds will need a plentiful and varied diet and both parents will feed the chicks. When first born they are tiny, naked little creatures and it will be about four weeks before they are fledged and begin to leave the nest and follow the parents to the feeding containers. At about six weeks they need to be separated from the parents so that the parents can lay again. At this age the young are fully able to support themselves but should be kept separate from the main colony.

Before the parents lay again the nest box should be thoroughly cleaned and disinfected to control the parasitic mites and other microscopic parasites that are present in even the most hygienic of colonies.

Budgerigars are a pleasing and inexpensive pet and the many varieties of them are very attractive. A flock in an outdoor aviary is a very attractive sight and they are vocal for most of the year. It is especially pleasant to watch them sitting and singing in the sun on their outdoor perches on a crisp winter's day with the snow on the ground! As with so many animals it is damp and chilling draughts that can cause harm rather than mere temperature and as long as they have warm and dry indoor accommodation the outside birds seem to flourish even better than those indoors. The proper care and management of a group of budgerigars and their rearing is not difficult to achieve but it does require attention to the techniques involved and also to the individual temperament and condition of each bird, and therefore represents a considerable achievement. The techniques and the lessons learnt in doing this will form an excellent basis for developing

a collection of other species. Accordingly, I feel that the budgerigar is one of the few small tropical birds that really can be recommended as a children's pet. I do hope, though, that if at all possible you will think about an outdoor aviary for a small group rather than a single bird indoors.

12 Horses and ponies

A horse or a pony is not a pet in the normal sense of the word because it is usually kept for a particular working purpose, in most cases for riding. Because of the interdependence of horse and rider the relationship between the two is inevitably a very close one and a horse or a pony is very much a part of the family. A horse or pony does not come into the usual category of children's pets but I am writing about them in this context because it is possible for many families to own them and there are a lot of traps for the first time owner to be wary of. This is therefore not intended as a complete guide to keeping a horse or a pony but as an explanation of some of the things that have to be taken into account.

Horses have been domesticated for over 6000 years and before the advent of steam power and later of the internal combustion engine they were the basis of the working and transport economy of the country. It is only in the last fifty years that the car and tractor have replaced the working horse. Since the 1950s there has been a rapid development of interest in the horse for riding as part of our leisure interests, and equestrian activities go from strength to strength. For anyone attracted to horses or ponies, whatever their age, there are ample facilities all over the country for learning to ride and for taking part in both competitive and non-competitive riding events. In addition one can show horses in hand and also drive them in harness. For most, though, there is the initial interest in riding a horse, and this can be followed up at a surprisingly reasonable cost at a local riding stable. If you think you are interested in riding this is the place to begin, and a short course of lessons will soon establish whether you are really interested or not. If the interest is strongly sustained you can take further lessons until you become proficient. You will then realise that a great deal is involved in looking after and riding a horse and that there is still a great deal more to be learnt! This doesn't mean lots of swotting but an open, lively mind that looks and listens and learns from more experienced people even if you don't see the point at the time! In this way a child can become as involved or not involved according to inclination. If you feel frightened or uncertain after having a few lessons then you may decide that riding is not for you.

The riding school will in most cases be able to cater for children to take part in events outside the school using the school's own horses and transport. At this stage it will still be cheaper to do it this way than to have your own horse.

It is the riding school that will have provided the basic grounding and knowledge of riding and horse care so that it is important to choose a good establishment from the outset where instruction is given only by qualified and experienced instructors, and pupils are not just allowed to slop around on a pony in a large class. A good school will normally be approved by or have the approval pending from the British Horse Society, and all establishments have to be licensed by the local authority, although the latter has absolutely nothing to do with the quality of the instruction or the standard of care of the horses. Approval by the BHS is very much concerned with these matters, and also the quality of the staff and facilities, safety precautions and so on. BHS approval is, however, a purely voluntary matter and there are good establishments which have not bothered to apply for inspection. When looking for a suitable riding stables write first to the British Horse Society, National Equestrian Centre, Stoneleigh, Warwickshire for their list of approved establishments and also for the address of your local branch of the Pony Club. The local secretary of this will be able to advise you in detail on all aspects of making a start with riding, and, being impartial, will get you started on the right lines and get you involved with the various activities run by the local branch at all levels of experience.

What of costs so far? These are fairly modest at this stage, being confined to the cost of lessons and riding, which will generally be £2–£3 an hour, and riding clothes. The latter should not be bought initially until you are sure that you wish to continue but thereafter basic riding clothes will be a must. A properly fitting hat is, however, a must from the start. Apart from the hat, riding clothes consist of jodphurs, jacket and jodphur boots or riding boots. You may also need a riding crop. The cost of this equipment varies greatly according to where you purchase them. Using the more moderately priced firms who specialise in riding wear they will cost you about £50, at 1978 prices. At the rate at which children grow out of riding clothes it is probably not worth paying the much higher prices of the more exclusive suppliers although generally their quality is such that for an adult they will last many years and are good value. Because of the cost of riding clothes there is a very considerable trade in out-grown riding clothes amongst pony club members and riding schools, so you may be able to acquire yours this way.

If you decide that you would like a horse or pony of your own you will need to consider several points very carefully. First of all what kind of horse should you be looking for, how big should it be, how old and what sort of experience should it have had? This is very much tied up with the purpose for which you want the horse, and your reasonable expectations of what you want to achieve with it. You won't win the Puissance at the Horse of the Year Show on a Shetland pony, for example! Secondly, you will need to consider the accommodation that is necessary for the horse or pony and how much work and exercise will be needed to keep it fit, and who will do this. Can these requirements be met locally? If you want to take part in competitions there is the question of getting you and the horse to and from them and finally the whole question of costs. The cost must take into account both the initial cost of getting started and thereafter running costs and incidental expenses.

It is very unlikely that you or your family will know enough to get you started properly and books alone will not be enough to save you from costly mistakes, especially in the choice and purchase of your first horse. Before your start get the detailed advice and assistance of an impartial person who has plenty of experience of horses and ponies. Your best approach is to contact your local branch of the Pony Club or the area representative of the British Horse Society. They should be able to suggest someone who can help, who may be a private individual, a dealer or riding school proprietor of recognised integrity. On the basis of their advice and their knowledge of your circumstances with regard to accommodation and so on they should be able to help you buy a horse or pony of the right size, and one with an appropriate temperament and level of performance to suit your abilities.

Your choice of breed or variety will very much depend on the accommodation which you have available. Whereas many of the native ponies, such as the Welsh and Exmoor, can live out for most of the year and require only a shelter for the worst weather, the finer kind of riding ponies may need to be kept in a stable for part of the year and to be exercised daily because of this. Each breed and cross has its own particular characteristics, and thus while Highland ponies are strong and steady animals which makes them ideal for trekking work they rarely have the speed and agility to do well in the jumping ring. Your first pony should not be a problem animal; he will need to be quiet, easy to handle and absolutely safe in traffic. The ideal first pony will often be described as a 'schoolmaster', which generally means that he has taught several people to ride who have then gone on to other ponies. The next stage on is described as a second pony, which means that it is not suitable for a beginner, needing more skill and experience to handle it safely. When looking for a pony be very careful where and how you buy. Do not buy a young pony (under five years old) unless you intend to have it broken and schooled professionally, and in which case it will almost certainly be intended as a second pony as there is no surer way of ruining a good pony and rider than letting a novice rider out on a young and inexperienced pony.

When looking at the descriptions of ponies at sales note both what is said about them and what is not said. The latter is the more significant. If the animal is not sold sound subject to veterinary examination then it is almost certainly not sound. If the description does not say that it is easy to catch and box, shoe, etc., then it won't be easy to handle and you will have problems. However, do be a little cautious with the descriptions, occasionally some very good horses and ponies are put into sales by people who know nothing about the finer points of description, and also when making an entry for a sale it is easy to omit something. So if you see a likely pony that is underdescribed then contact the owner and ask specifically about those points and arrange to see and try the pony before the sale. Sales vary greatly in their quality and any sale is always an opportunity for a breeder or owner to dispose of animals that they would not wish to sell with a full personal warranty. At a sale it is a case of let the buyer beware and the onus is on him to establish whether the animal is suitable for his purpose, although the descriptions given in the details of the sale and those given verbally by the auctioneer in his description of the animal are legally binding. Good animals are entered in the better horse sales and it is an easy matter to check the reputation of a particular sale, and also to pick out from the catalogue the better entries. The problem with sales is that unless you can contact the owner beforehand there is only a limited opportunity of looking at and trying out the horses.

The most satisfactory way of buying a horse or a pony is by a private sale when the buyer has ample opportunity to look at and try the animal, and can sometimes, if suitable facilities are available for the care of the horse, take it on a week's trial if they are seriously intending to buy it. The purpose of the trial period is to ascertain fully that the animal is suitable as described. Whilst I insist on this for animals which I am buying I am often less than keen to allow my animals away for trial to people and places which I do not know. You must, therefore, consider the position of the person selling the pony. A poor performance by the pony is often the fault of the rider, and the buyer might be better served by having the child spend several sessions with the pony on its home ground under supervision to fully reveal its performance. There have been occasions when we have refused to sell a pony to a family because we judged that the child could not properly cope with it. In a private sale you have ample opportunity to try and make up your mind about the animal, as well as to have it inspected by a veterinary surgeon. In addition, a private sale implies also that the seller is personally warranting the suitability of the animal, and a private breeder or owner is much less likely to harm their reputation by selling a dud animal, but do beware still because there are plenty of people who will do anything or tell you anything in their enthusiasm to sell a horse. Do bear in mind that in selling a horse a fair description must be given by the owner, and that answers to specific questions are part of the contract of sale, and if incorrect or misleading are grounds for returning the animal or receiving compensation.

In buying a horse or pony you will only get what you pay for when you buy an animal that is of an age to have shown its abilities and qualities. The question of price is always a difficult one and the only conclusion that I have come to is that you will have to pay a good price for a good animal, which should also of course be regarded as a good investment that will command an appropriate price if resold when it is outgrown. Good horses and ponies are in short supply and when one considers the cost of breeding and breaking them in even the best ones seem comparatively inexpensive. There is a fair price for every animal and you will need to look accordingly, but as a very rough guide, you are unlikely to buy a good pony for under £200 and it could well cost you a lot more than that.

If at all possible you should have a field in which your horse or pony can be kept along with a companion or at least in which they can be turned out during the day. Each pony needs a minimum of 0.8 hectares (2 acres) if kept out in a field. If you have a hardy native pony then a simple field shelter will generally be sufficient housing all year round. For any of the non-native types it will be necessary to have a proper stable for about six months of the year and also for odd occasions at other times. Horses do not like being kept on their own and if you do put one in a field by itself you will almost certainly have trouble with it jumping out, especially if other horses go by. In doing so it is likely to injure itself and may well cause other damage or an accident. You will normally need to come to an arrangement with someone for a couple of companion animals which is not difficult to arrange. The ideal system in which to keep a horse in a field is where the grazing can be shared with both cattle and sheep so that the grass is evenly grazed and parasites are reduced by the mutual grazing. In the winter the field will not normally supply sufficient food for the stock and additional feeding will have to be supplied. If at all possible the field should be periodically rested to avoid damage to the grass.

Although there are plenty of fields around horses are very unpopular as grazers with many farmers. For this reason you may not find it easy to obtain grazing. If you are unable to make any arrangements for grazing and shelter the alternative is for the pony to be kept at a professional stables on a livery system, that is, one where you pay for the horse to be looked after. Various arrangements can be worked out for livery so that the cost will vary, and one possibility is for the horse to do some work in the riding school and to have the bill reduced accordingly. Livery charges are not cheap, reflecting as they do the cost of labour, feed and shelter. The situation does, however, vary considerably from place to place, and you should make exhaustive enquiries in your neighbourhood for possible suitable accommodation. You may be surprised what turns up.

One of the greatest problems is to keep your pony properly exercised during the week or the school terms so that it is sufficiently fit to perform at the weekend or during the school holidays. Careful feeding and exercise are essential and if the pony is kept in it should be ridden or walked daily, though if kept out being ridden every two days should be sufficient to keep it fit. This level of exercise is sufficient for general fitness but is not enough to get your pony into condition for competitive cross-country events or for hunting.

During the summer if the pony is kept at grass only a little supplementary feeding may be necessary. Some ponies become overfat on grass and you may have to keep the pony in for part of the time to cut down the amount of grass being eaten. No horse or pony should be allowed to get fat and overweight, at the very least it is an extra strain on the horse which can have damaging effects in the long term or cause it to founder. The legs suffer because of the excess weight or it may develop laminitis. The only cure for obesity is less food and more exercise. The pony which is kept in will require a regular supply of hay together with an energy food such as oats, sugar beet pulp, crushed barley and similar cereals together with bran. Alternatively, ponies can be accustomed to a partial or total diet of pellet foods. Your feeding programme and schedule will depend on the time of year, how the pony is kept, the amount of work that it is doing, and the range of food that you can conveniently supply. In addition to his food a stabled horse will require straw for bedding, although shredded newspaper and wood shavings (not sawdust) or peat are now being used as alternatives to straw.

When you are keeping a horse you also have the problem of storing its food and bedding, and this raises a new factor of costs versus convenience against facilities available. Straw, hay and cereals become available during the summer and early autumn, and the cheapest way to obtain them is to collect the hay and straw off the field yourself, or alternatively to have a load delivered off the field. Once it has been taken into the farm for storage its price goes up and if you buy it through a contractor again the price and the transport costs increase and you may only be able to purchase it in ten-tonne loads. Equally, for every week you go into winter the price keeps going up especially if it looks like being a bad winter. Hay and straw must be kept dry and shed or barn storage is desirable, failing which you will need to make a stack and to protect it with a heavy gauge plastic rick sheet which is not all that expensive.

Cereals are more difficult as these need to be stored whole and then crushed for feeding. Crushed oats go stale after a couple of weeks so you don't normally want more than a 100kg (2 cwt) of bruised oats about. They should be stored in a lidded bin or a closed sack. Unless you are able to make a special arrangement with a local farmer to supply you say with 500kg ($\frac{1}{2}$ ton) of bruised oats collected by the sack as needed you will have to obtain them from an agricultural merchant as you will the others items mentioned. It does, of course, work out dearer that way and prices do fluctuate, on the other hand you don't have to pay out so much in one go. There is nothing like a year's bill for hay, straw and oats at the beginning of October to start a heated family discussion!

The price of hay and straw will vary greatly from area to area and from year to year. At the moment (1978) with a reasonable harvest one expects to pay about £30-50 for good quality hay per tonne. Bad hay is worthless at any price, and straw costs about £15 per tonne. Oats are about £80 per tonne. Your actual needs depend on so many different factors that you cannot give an estimate of cost without knowing the horse and the circumstances. I reckon that our 11.2 hands high Welsh pony which lives out all year requires about a tonne of hay and about 250kg (5 cwt) of concentrates (oats, pellets, sugar beet etc.) which costs about £100 a year. In the summer hay and concentrates are negligible except for when he is brought in to prepare for a competition. On the other hand, our 15.1 hands high riding horse requires about two tonnes of hay, 500kg ($\frac{1}{2}$ ton) of concentrates and about 1524kg (30 cwt) of straw for bedding being kept in at night: a cost of around £160 for winter feed with only a small amount of hay and concentrates in the summer, the cost of summer feeding being the cost of your own grazing. With the problems of obtaining and storing hay and straw at harvest time, and the progressive increase in price, especially for small quantities, as time goes by, comes the question of whether a commercial complete diet might be easier to cope with, and also whether there is an alternative to straw bedding. A complete pellet food, fed according to the manufacturer's instructions, will keep your horse fit and well. Its great advantage is that it can be bought by the bag as required and is of standardised food value. Pellets are more expensive than hay and concentrates but when everything is taken into account the cost difference is probably going to be quite small and if their convenience is the answer to your storage or other problems with bulk foods or high prices then these could well be the basis of your feeding programme. Do, though, add some titbits to counteract the monotony! And always make sure that plenty of water is available. Convenience also applies to the question of bedding and since shredded paper, peat and shavings are now available in commercial packs protected by polythene they can be stacked outside without any need for shelter.

If you are considering the purchase of a stable or the conversion of an existing building there are a number of things to take into account. A children's pony requires a room measuring about 3.5 metres (10 ft) square with a height of not less than about 2.75 metres (9 ft.) A larger horse will need not less than 3.65 metres (12 ft) square to have full mobility. A stable type of door, that is one with an opening top half, is required so that the horse can look out in fine weather. The whole box must be adequately ventilated and also well drained. Local planning authorities have planning and building requirements for stables and you will need to comply with these. A very popular way is to purchase a sectional timber stable and to have this put up on a convenient site. These are in general also subject to planning and building controls. They are available from a great many manufacturers in different parts of the country and the prices vary considerably according to the type of material used, its thickness and quality and the standard of workmanship. The biggest pitfall with these is the thickness and quality of the wood and its preservation and finish. Horses are powerful creatures and the thin wood used in some of the cheaper boxes will not stand up to either the horses or to the weather for very long. Basically if you are looking at the cheaper end of the range you will have to study the specification most carefully and do not hesitate to ask the firm for an address where you can go and see one of the boxes. The more expensive and widely

A typical sectional-built stable

advertised boxes are generally of very good quality and in the long run are an excellent investment. Ideally one might buy in the middle price range a box that has many of the features of the more expensive ones.

If you have bought your own pony you will need to buy the tack to go with it. This means the saddle and bridle, head collar, blankets, rugs, grooming kit and so on. This is a major capital outlay and you will do well to buy good quality items carefully because the price of an identical item can vary considerably between shops and dealers, and also because if well looked after your tack will keep its value and thus may be regarded as an investment. Your tack must fit your pony and should be bought for that particular pony. The most important item is the saddle which must be fitted carefully. A good saddler will bring a selection of saddles to fit these to the horse and rider, equally, if you have a good show in your neighbourhood, especially a county show, there will usually be a number of saddlery stalls there and you could take your pony along. This would give you a chance of comparing qualities and prices. I would suggest that you take a knowledgeable person with you to help to sort out the relative qualities and prices. At 1978 prices you should be able to buy a reasonably good English saddle for about £100 where there is reasonable competition between dealers. The identical saddle might cost you considerably more in a larger store or expensive shop. Saddles can be bought secondhand, but they must be in good condition and not have the panels worn, the stuffing slipping or worn out or, far more seriously, the tree broken. (The tree is the framework upon which the saddle is built.) Only buy a secondhand saddle that is in good condition for a fair price if it fits properly. An old saddle in bad condition is no good and is likely to cost you a lot of money to have it repaired. All in all the basic tack for the horse or pony is going to cost at least £200 at present prices. There is always a steady flow of minor items for replacements and any child who has a horse or pony will generally have a shopping list of wants that can be made discreetly known as birthdays or Christmas come near.

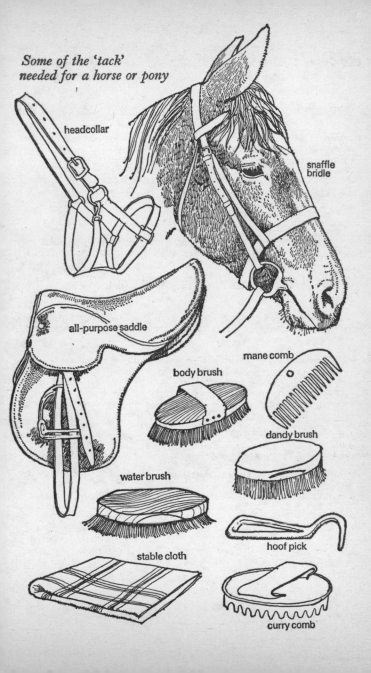

Some of the 'tack' needed for a horse or pony

headcollar

snaffle bridle

all-purpose saddle

body brush

mane comb

dandy brush

water brush

hoof pick

stable cloth

curry comb

If you are really keen to have a horse or pony of your own and are prepared to carry out the hard work that is required to look after and exercise it, and won't get bored with it after a few months, then you should discuss it with your family because it is going to affect everyone. Between you you should be able to work out whether it is possible to have a pony of your own or whether you can continue with your interest through a riding school, friend or neighbour. It is not only the matter of whether you can afford the initial purchase, equipping and running cost of your pony, but also whether there are suitable facilities for keeping it and also whether the family can cope with the demands that a pony in the family makes on everyone's life. If you do have a pony then you may find that there are some other things that you will have to sacrifice for it but it is a very worthwhile and enjoyable animal to have. But do go into it very carefully first, and above all do get expert help and advice from the start.

13 Reptiles and amphibians

Opinions vary on the general suitability of reptiles and amphibians as pets for children. Certain of these two groups, notably newts and the tadpoles of frogs and toads (amphibians), and tortoises (reptiles) are very widely kept. Many of these animals are not difficult to keep in captivity once certain basic requirements of accommodation and feeding have been met and several children I know look after a variety of reptiles and amphibians very well. My main concern with them as pets for children lies in the fact that it is not possible to have the same degree of rapport with a toad or a snake that there can be between birds and mammals and their owners. There are few people who would not recognise the symptoms of simple illness or that all was not well with a mammal; few would be able to do this with a reptile or amphibian until the condition became more serious. For this reason only a very few reptiles or amphibians should be considered as first pets for children, the rest, I feel should be restricted to the established pet keeper or enthusiastic family who will be able to look after them properly.

The most generally suitable accommodation for reptiles and amphibians is a glass aquarium tank planted or landscaped according to the needs of the particular species. It is most important that this is furnished correctly otherwise the animals will not flourish. The top of the tank should be covered with a flyproof fine gauze mesh and above this can be fitted lamps according to the type of environment that is to be maintained. Amphibians in general require moist conditions and the tropical ones will need to be warm as well as damp to produce a high humidity (water content of the air) inside the tank. This high humidity for the tropical amphibians can be produced by having a sheet of thin glass fitted about 5mm above the gauze mesh with the necessary heat provided by electric light bulbs in a hood over the glass. As these will need to be switched off at night without greatly altering the humidity it may be preferrable to have the temperature and humidity controlled by means of a heated pool within the tank using submersible aquarium heaters. Our native frogs, toads and newts will not require additional heat and the tank should be arranged so as to include a pool in which they can submerge, a good area of moist peat and moss into which they can burrow and a smaller area of drier habitat.

The reason for having a well-fitting fine mesh lid to the aquarium is that the principal food of amphibians is live insects and the most practical way of providing this is by breeding flies. Amphibians will ignore dead food so that any insects must be released live into the tank for them to hunt. The skin of an amphibian is delicate and needs to be kept in good condition as they also breathe through it. Of our native amphibians I have found toads to be by far the most engaging and tame. Certainly for handling they are the most suitable.

Reptiles are also in most cases best kept in an aquarium tank or comparable structure, planted and landscaped according to the needs of the species being kept. Like the amphibians the reptiles cannot regulate their body temperature, and take on that of the surroundings. According to the temperature they may be very active, when it is warm, or very sluggish when it is much cooler. The temperature at which reptiles are kept must therefore be carefully controlled within the range that they would normally experience in their environment, bearing in mind, though, that they do modify this to avoid the extremes, by, for example, burrowing during the day to escape the extremes of heat from the sun and also at night to avoid the cold. The humidity at which reptiles should be kept varies considerably between species. Some like it warm and moist but many are better kept in drier conditions irrespective of the temperature. Many lizards

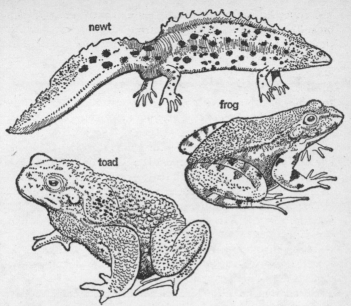

*Native amphibians which can be encouraged in
garden pools*

enjoy basking in the sun and will use the heat from a light
bulb for this.

Most reptiles, particulary lizards and the like, require a
mixed diet of fruit, vegetables and insects although some will
feed almost exclusively on one or the other. One group of
reptiles, the snakes, mostly feed on live animals. The common grass snake, for example, feeds on insects and young
frogs, whilst pythons catch rats and mice. It is not easy to
accustom snakes to feed on dead food even when freshly
killed, or even to feed in captivity at all. Snakes are very
sensitive creatures and are upset by a change in their environment or by unfamiliar handling. The keeping and
management of snakes is very much an art and is not to be
undertaken lightly.

A number of aquatic reptiles, mostly young terrapins, have

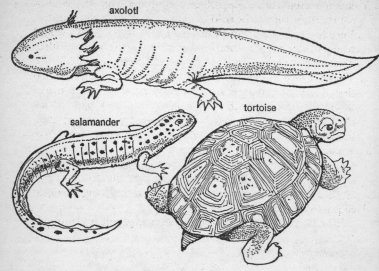

axolotl

salamander

tortoise

Some interesting reptiles

been imported in recent years and these can be kept quite
adequately in an indoor tank in which they are provided with
a gently shelving 'beach' on which they can haul out of the
water. Another very interesting animal which is suitable as
a pet is an axolotl. An axolotl is the tadpole stage of a land-
dwelling lizard, the Mexican salamander. The salamander
gives birth to live tadpoles which grow to about 20cm (8 in) in
length and look like large newts with gills. Many of these will
spend their whole life at this stage of development but they
can be induced to change into the adult salamander sometimes just by providing an area on which they can haul out of
the water, or failing this, by gradually lowering the water
level in the tank so that the axolotl can no longer immerse
itself and cannot easily use its gills, and instead breathes with
its lungs. This should be done over something like a three-
week period.

The most widely kept reptile and probably the most
abused pet of all is the tortoise. Every year these are shipped

in large quantities in appalling conditions from the wild in southern Europe to be sold in pet stores all over the country. Very few of them survive until the next summer and I would frankly like to see their importation strictly controlled. Tortoises are plant feeders and are also very partial to fruit. They are also wanderers. If your garden is securely enclosed then during the summer a pet tortoise can be given the run of the garden from which it will select a variety of food including many flower heads. They favour fine young grasses, tender leaves of lettuce and dandelion, and also fruits like tomatoes, bananas and finely sliced apple. If you cannot give your tortoise the freedom of the garden a portable enclosure should be provided. They must have protection from the sun as they do not like extremes of temperature, and at night require to be indoors or well protected.

The best time to purchase tortoises is about midsummer

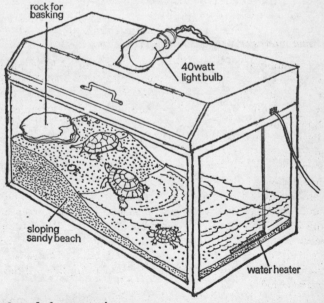

rock for basking

40 watt light bulb

sloping sandy beach

water heater

A tank for terrapins

when they will have had the chance to feed for several months in the wild before capture. In this way they will have some reserves of food left to cover them whilst they are settling in. Tortoises are quite sociable animals and if at all possible a true pair should be purchased as there is a possibility, in time, of breeding from them, and they seem to appreciate company. Before buying, examine each animal carefully and select one whose shell is in good condition, who is not cut or damaged around the body and has clear eyes and no signs of a running nose or weeping eyes. Tortoises are long-lived animals and if you look after yours carefully and ensure that they are able to hibernate properly you should be able to keep them for many years. Tortoises begin to hibernate in response to the falling temperature of autumn. Before you allow a tortoise to hibernate it is important to make sure that it is well fed and has enough body reserves to last it through the hibernation period. If it hasn't it will die without waking up as the only thing that will bring a tortoise out of hibernation is a rising temperature. The very small tortoises will not survive hibernation and these should be kept indoors and fed through the winter. When the tortoises show signs of hibernating and are well fed they should be placed in a large wooden box well packed with straw or leaf mould, and the box put in a cool place that is not subject to a greatly fluctuating temperature and which is protected from frost. In the spring the tortoise will normally awaken naturally or can be encouraged to do so by placing the box in a warmer place. Do, however, allow its awakening to take place gently. When awakened the eyes, nose and skin can be gently cleaned and wiped and food and water provided.

Tortoises have had a very bad deal from man and if you do decide to keep a pair do try and make a good job of it. Reptiles and amphibians are also animals that are unfamiliar to many of us and are a very misunderstood group. I would like to see them more widely kept as pets as they are of great interest in their own right and anyone familiar with them soon realises what a lot of nonsense is talked and written about them.

14 Aquarium life

The keeping of tanks of fish has become increasingly popular in recent years and it is not difficult to appreciate why this is so. A fish tank can be a very attractive item in a room and for a very small amount of space will house a variety of colourful and active fish. When correctly set up a fish tank needs little maintenance and it is possible to leave a tank of fish with food for several days without causing any harm or cruelty. The further reason is that aquarium technology and technique have greatly improved so that a first class display can be set up and maintained at a relatively low cost even by a beginner.

I would like to look at two levels of keeping an aquarium, one concerned with pond life, the second with tropical fish. Both of these are freshwater systems and I regard a marine aquarium as too advanced to be undertaken without proven skill in maintaining a tropical freshwater one, unless of course it is mum or dad who has got the bug!

A tremendous variety of fascinating animals are to be found in lakes and ponds and all of these can be kept and studied in a cold water aquarium or even in a home-made or bought pool. It is possible to keep pond creatures in washing up bowls but an aquarium tank has the advantage that you can see and watch the inhabitants more closely through the glass sides. It is true, however, that those pond creatures which shun the light will then go and hide amongst the weed so you won't see them very easily, but for many of the creatures the side light seems to have little effect and for some like leeches and snails the sides of the tank are often used as an anchorage or for feeding. There are two kinds of aquarium which you can buy, either glass or plastic. The plastic ones are cheaper and less likely to break but do become scratched with time. The glass ones do not scratch and in theory are more likely to get broken, though in practice it is unlikely that this will happen. In practice, any long term aquarium set-up should always use a glass tank, while the plastic ones can be used to advantage for shorter term projects. For any situation you should buy the largest tank which you can accommodate or afford as its volume relates directly to the number of species which can be kept and the total number of all species which the system can support.

A pond life tank can be simply set up using some of the water from the pool together with the plants. You should try and reconstruct as best you can the habitat of the pool from which you are collecting. Any pool habitat contains a mixture of predators and their prey and unless you remove some of the predators, such as the great diving beetles and the dragonfly nymphs, your other species will gradually be killed off. For this reason you may wish to set up a number of subsidiary tanks to accommodate separately the predatory species which you will, of course, have to feed.

A tank suitable for pond life

The cycle in the pond is very much a seasonal one and through the year many of your inhabitants will change into adult forms and leave. Some species such as the newts are only temporary inhabitants of the water and would normally hibernate on land. Their young, for example, will not return to the water for several years until they are fully grown and mature and ready to breed, the same is true of frogs and toads so you will need to plan for the release of your pool stock in plenty of time for them to prepare themselves for the winter. The best way of doing this is to return them in August or September, if not earlier, to the pool from which they were collected. It is possible to keep some of these creatures permanently in captivity but it does require a lot of skill and know-how to do it properly.

If you are interested in a particular species such as the stickleback or newt it is advisable to set up a tank specifically for them so that conditions will be just right. In this way it is possible to observe the courtship of these fascinating creatures and to follow the development of their young. In any such set-up the number of individuals should be restricted and the area must be carefully planted up with the correct plants that will provide cover and protection for the eggs and later for the young. It is also necessary to ensure that the correct food is available for the species and since these are both predatory on small worms and pond creatures, such as daphnia, much of this can be supplied as live food in the tank.

To my mind there is no better way to introduce a child to the fascination of wildlife than by encouraging him or her to collect and set up a tank of pond life. Do, however, remember that lakes and ponds can be very dangerous places so take an adult with you when you go to collect your specimens. All that is required for collecting is a strong net, some stout polythene bags and a couple of buckets. The best way of transporting the creatures home is to put them in bags of water with plenty of weed and then to tie the neck of the bag. The bags are then placed in the buckets for ease of carrying. At home each bag can be tipped out into a bowl and its inhabitants lifted out with a spoon into the permanent tank.

Tropical freshwater fish are in most cases brightly coloured and attractive to look at so that a tank of them is not only a home but a very attractive setting as well. If you are thinking about setting up a tropical tank, first of all visit a specialist aquarium supplier to get an idea of the range of stock available and the equipment required, together with its cost. The main items are the tank itself, possibly a tank stand, small electrical heaters and a thermostat, a thermometer, filtration equipment and an aerating pump. Filtration and aeration will enable you to accommodate far more fish in the tank than would otherwise be the case, and also to keep them without having to worry too much about the chemical balance in the tank. You should read a specialist book about actually setting up your tank but the basic principles remain. An under-gravel filtration system will keep your water clean and free of noxious substances by having them broken down by bacteria in the gravel layer. It will also keep down the amount of fine particles in the water that would otherwise make it look very cloudy. The filter plates are set up in the base of the tank before the fine gravel is added. A column leaves the filter and is connected to the electric pump which circulates the water through the filters and also bubbles air through the water to maintain the oxygen content. Heaters controlled by a thermostat are located just above the gravel, generally on the back wall of the tank a few centimetres from each end. They are electrical heaters enclosed in a glass tube with a rating of about 60 watts. Two heaters are used, controlled by a thermostat, so that if one fails the other is capable of maintaining the temperature.

A tank should be set up about a week before any fish are to be put in it. With the gravel in place over the filter plates the water is added and the bottom of the tank gently landscaped so that it falls away from back to front. Some pieces of well-washed rock, preferably hard igneous rock like granite that will not dissolve in the water, are added as landscape features. The heaters and the thermostat are now put in place and switched on, together with the aerator which is also providing the suction for the filter. It will take several days for

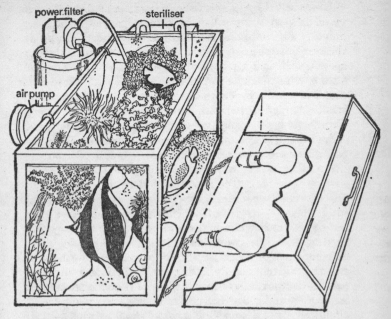

A tropical aquarium with its hood removed

the water to balance out to its correct temperature which should be about 78° Fahrenheit. When this is reached according to the temperature indicated by the tank thermometer, the thermostat should be adjusted accordingly. Plants are an essential part of the life system of the aquarium and they will need light for about fourteen hours per day. This is supplied by electric light bulbs above the tank. The precise amount of light needed and the duration of it can be calculated from a simple formula. The lights are usually housed in a hood which fits over the aquarium. They become hot, and it is necessary to protect them against water splash and also to prevent evaporation with a sheet of glass, which must not cut out the air supply to the water surface. The heat from the lamps will often raise the water temperature above that of the thermostat so that when the lights are on the heaters will often be off. Lights should not be switched on and off suddenly from darkness to light and vice versa as fish are very prone to shock. In the normal course of things the lights should be switched on and off while there is natural light to smooth the transition, alternatively a dimmer switch can be fitted to a time control so that the light is faded in and out. Lights should not be left on all the time as fish have rhythms like other animals, in which day and night are important. They are in most habitats also subject to some fall in water temperature at night and the drop that will occur when the lights go out is positively beneficial to them.

Plants are important in an aquarium, not only for decorative purposes, but to provide places there fish can hide and shelter, and also to remove carbon dioxide from the water and add oxygen. The roots of the plants feed on the nutrients released by the bacteria in the under-gravel filtration system from waste matter produced by the fish. There are many different kinds of plants that can be grown in a tropical tank and these will root readily in the gravel and as long as there is a sufficient output of light from the lamps should appear green and healthy and grow vigorously. The light supplied should be entirely artificial and should not be supplemented by sunlight from one side as the plants will then tend to grow towards this. Because the plant growth is so vigorous plants will have to be regularly cut back otherwise they will form a dense mat on the surface and all the plants below will die because the light has been shut out. Plants should be allowed to grow upwards but not to spread themselves out over the surface. For the same reasons, surface-dwelling plants should be avoided and any flat-leaved plants should be kept at a low level within the tank. The plants should be added once the temperature of the tank has settled down, and a few days later the fish can be added.

Fish should only be bought from a reputable aquarist firm or reliable private breeder to ensure that they are free of disease. Not all species are compatible with each other and you should check before buying which will settle together. I would suggest that a few species be purchased first and introduced to the tank as a test that all is well. It is better to lose a few than the whole lot because something is wrong, perhaps through contamination. When introducing fish the bags containing them should be lowered into the tank and left for some hours to adjust to its temperature. The fish can then be released into it. Some initial losses are to be expected but the tank should settle down quite readily. If it doesn't, get expert advice from your supplier or local aquarist society.

Really excellent commercial feeds are available for all different kinds of fish and regular supplies of live food can be purchased from aquarist shops so there should be no problem in feeding the fish. Most common ailments such as white spot fungus can now be treated with proprietary medicines so that health is much less of a problem than it was in the past. Once your tank is set up, though, do be careful about introducing additional fish in case you bring in an infection with them.

There is a great deal of information and many excellent books available on how to keep aquarium fish, and it is as well to read a number of these to get a good background to the setting up and management of your tank and also the variety of stock that is available. I would also recommend joining your local aquarist society whose members will be able to give you a great deal of help and advice when first setting up your tank, and also with any problems that may occur.

15 Insects

It is now relatively straightforward to obtain the eggs of many British and foreign butterflies, moths and other kinds of insect, and to rear and breed them in captivity. A most valuable side effect from this is the possibility of breeding and releasing into the wild many of our native butterflies which have become increasingly scarce in the countryside due to the destruction of the plants on which they feed and because of the widespread use of chemical sprays. It is possible to rear these insects, whether you have a suitable garden in which they can be reared on their food plants, or in a city flat, in which case you gather the food plant and feed it to them. It is important to stress, however, that although you can buy foreign species these should not be released in the wild. Our climate is quite unsuitable for most of them and they are unlikely to survive. There is also the possibility of introducing a new pest species, and our native wildlife has got enough problems without any more introductions.

Worldwide Butterflies Limited, of Sherborne, Dorset, specialise in the supply of insect stock and all the necessary rearing equipment and literature. I would advise you first of all to obtain a copy of their catalogue and price list and then to order some of the relevant information from them. If you do decide to go ahead you can order the species and few simple pieces of equipment which you will need. I would like to think that our pet enthusiasts would make a start with some of our native butterflies because they do need our assistance to survive and it is only by individual efforts that they will. You will see how simple it is in your garden to give them what they need by leaving a small area uncultivated and planting it with suitable food plants such as stinging nettle and dandelion. You can also encourage a magnificent display of butterflies by planting a butterfly bush, a species of buddleia whose sweet blossom attracts many beautiful butterflies and other insects to feed, to the great benefit of the garden as a whole. If your family are keen gardeners you can assure them that your butterflies will not be eating all their flowers and vegetables!

To begin with, ensure that there will be enough of the required food plant available, which should not be a problem as mostly quite common species can be used. You then order the eggs which will come as they were laid on a suitable food plant. When they hatch they can either be transferred as tiny caterpillars to a potted food plant or on to that plant outside. To avoid harming them a fine brush can be used for handling and so that they will not escape or be eaten by birds a fine muslin bag is tied over the plant so as to totally enclose them. When fully fed and grown the caterpillars turn into chrysalids where they undergo the change into butterflies or moths and from which they will later emerge as perfect adults. It depends on the species whether the butterflies will emerge that season or the following year and this will affect how you store them. Those that will emerge this season are left to harden for a few days and then transferred on to peat, paper or other material according to their requirements in a simple gauze cage in which the butterfly will emerge and climb up a twig to spread and dry its wings. The chrysalids should be sprayed gently to keep them moist. Species that will not emerge until the following year can be kept in plastic boxes in a dark cool place and be transferred to the emerging cage at the appropriate time.

When the adults have emerged they will soon seek a mate, and if they are kept in a breeding cage you will be able to have your stock lay a new generation of eggs on the appropriate food plant, whilst hopefully those that you have liberated will have done likewise and will be laying their eggs on appropriate food plants in the garden. You will have to make sure that

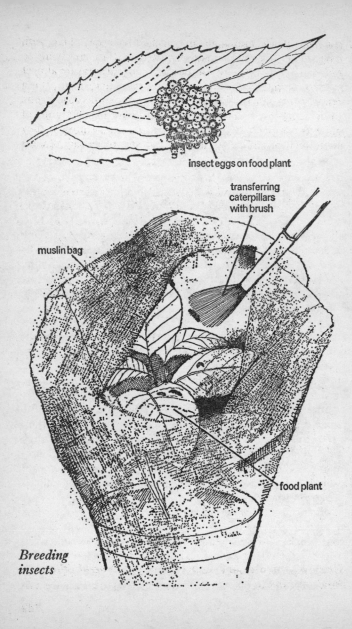

insect eggs on food plant

transferring caterpillars with brush

muslin bag

food plant

Breeding insects

the rest of the family do not accidently spray them with insecticide. It is unfortunate that gardeners are now being so indoctrinated that there is a specific chemical spray for almost everything that might ever settle on a gardener's plant. It is a tragedy that this has been allowed to happen because at one time it looked as if our gardens could have become some of our most important nature reserves. As it is at present they could well become a sterile gaudy desert of waving blooms

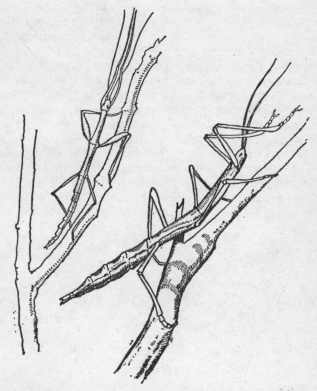

Stick insects are very easy to keep and several different kinds are available

unless our gardeners stop the widespread use of these deadly poisons.

Another favourite insect pet is the stick insect. Many different varieties of these are now available and they are very easy to keep and breed. The principal food plant for them in captivity is privet. All that is required to keep them is an enclosed container with a fine muslin lid to stop them escaping. This contains a jar of water in which sprigs of privet stand. The cage should be lined with sand. The insects spend their time on the twigs and leaves and can devour them quite rapidly. They lay eggs which soon hatch into miniatures of their parents about four millimetres long and grow rapidly. The privet is consumed very quickly and with a good colony going will need to be replaced daily.

Insects certainly are very rewarding and a great deal of very beautiful and unusual ones from all over the world are now available to be reared in captivity, and it is very worthwhile attempting this as both the stock and the equipment are inexpensive. The good that you can do for your local butterfly situation should encourage you to have a go at helping some of our native wildlife, but do remember that it is wild habitat that will ultimately be required for the descendants of your stock, so plan to have some of this ready for them too.

16 Wild animals as pets

Very few of our native wild animals are suitable for keeping as pets and I wouldn't list any of them as being a suitable pet for a child. A number of wild animals do, however, turn up quite regularly, either injured, or as apparently orphaned youngsters. If these can be looked after and successfully reared it is a very interesting and rewarding experience but you should attempt it only if you have sufficient accommodation of the right kind for them or if you can release them back into the wild.

Many of the allegedly orphaned animals which are picked up by people are not orphans at all, it being part of the normal pattern of parental care for the youngster to be left alone away from the adults. Also, many young birds which are not yet able to fly are being fed by the parent birds. If you pick up one of these youngsters you then have the very difficult task of feeding and caring for it. Some, such as jackdaws, are not very difficult to rear and are friendly inquisitive birds which when reared and released may well choose to stay around the home; others, such as swallows, are more difficult to rear and the problem comes when in the autumn they seek to migrate. It should also be emphasised that it is illegal to take most of our native birds into captivity although nobody is going to arrest you for looking after a small bird. If, however, this is a bird of prey you would be well advised to inform your local police station what you are doing and of the circumstances in which you acquired the bird. The reason for this is that increasingly birds of prey are being stolen as eggs and chicks from the wild to be trained for hawking and falconry, and anyone found in illegal possession of these birds is liable to prosecution.

One of the commonest finds of the larger birds are young owls, mostly tawny owls which breed and live in close proximity to man and are often found on the ground away from any visible nest. At this stage they are generally moulting from a very fluffy set of baby feathers to a more adult plumage. They are not difficult to rear on a diet of mice, dead day old chicks, and road casualty rabbits. It is very important that they receive the whole carcass so that they get meat and fur as well. The indigestible bone and fur is subsequently regurgitated through the mouth in the form of a pellet. All birds of prey, and many others, also do this. Carefully handled, a young owl will become very tame, but if left unhandled to any great extent it will grow up appropriately cautious. It is not easy to rehabilitate owls into the wild as they have to be taught to catch live food and to hunt for themselves. Expert assistance is required. If the owl is to be kept it is essential that it be kept tame so that it can be flown for exercise, and that it has appropriate accommodation. For an owl or any other bird of prey that is to be kept you would be advised to study carefully a textbook on falconry which deals with the accommodation, housing and training of predatory birds, and to seek assistance from an experienced falconer; in this way the bird can be properly cared for. An alternative, and one that I use with injured adults when they are recovered from their injury and if they cannot be released into the wild again, is to pair them up with a similar injured or damaged bird in captivity and to try and breed from them. This has in the past been surprisingly successful, the only problem being that owls are extremely difficult to sex with certainty.

Injured birds which you may come across or have brought to you are very difficult to deal with and in accepting such an animal you have a very clear responsibility either to rehabilitate or to painlessly destroy it, since in the wild most injured creatures would die or be killed within a matter of hours. Injuries which are visible are generally only a part of the story which usually includes internal damage as well. A

A wild bird feeding its young

simple broken wing or a leg is one thing, multiple injuries from a car collision are a very different matter. In either case expert veterinary assistance is called for and this will almost always involve an X-ray to establish the extent of bone damage. Once treated by the vet you can apply your skills to nursing and caring for the animal.

Deer fawns, especially those of roe deer, are regularly picked up by the public during the main fawning months of May and June and hardly any of them are genuine orphans. If in the wild you come across a deer fawn do not touch it. Admire it and leave so that the mother can return. If it squeaks at you and tries to follow you ignore it and go away, it will be wanting its mother whom you are keeping away. It is just possible that it might be a real orphan, so make a careful note of the spot where you saw it and inform the local warden/

gamekeeper/forester of what you saw so that he can later make a check. If you don't know who this is, the local police station will. Deer do not make family pets, I know this very well because for many years we kept and bred several kinds of deer. It was a fascinating experience and we learnt a lot from them. I should like to do it again, but not until I can afford enough ground, fencing and so on to be able to keep them properly on their own terms. There is nothing more pathetic or sickening to my mind than the usual orphan 'bambi' reared against all odds for its survival on tea and cornflakes or other bizarre diet. At six months they are about the size they would normally have been at six weeks, with weak wobbly legs, thin and with a poor coat and they often spend their lives tethered by a collar or shut in a shed for much of the time. At such times I am reminded of the words of Blake about caged robin; 'all heaven in a rage'. Young deer are not easy to rear well, as only ten per cent of those picked up will live beyond a week without skilled and knowledgeable care and of these, without proper facilities (and that includes many zoos and wildlife parks) few will grow up into adults comparable with those living wild. Fawns if more than a few days old will not tame to any significant extent. Tame or semi-tame male deer lose their fear of man and in the breeding season become aggressive and exceedingly dangerous. Every year several people are killed by tame male deer kept as pets and zoo keepers rightly regard them as more dangerous than the big cats.

In spring there are usually a number of fox cubs on offer. These have generally been obtained by farmers or keepers digging an earth after killing the vixen and then taking pity on the cubs. Foxes can make very interesting pets if you are lucky enough to have one with a very good temperament, to have got it at the right age, to have really made a pet of it with the family from the start. You must also have suitable outdoor accommodation for when it is older, and the time to give it a couple of hours exercise and play each day, a very demanding list but an essential one for a fine, fit and healthy fox. Most fall short of this in some measure and this is where the problems can begin. Once you have taken on a fox cub you must see it through to the point of release or of keeping it all its life because very few zoos or wildlife parks want to know about tame foxes. If your fox is very tame you should keep it or find someone with an enthusiasm for them who can take it on. If, at about six months, it is not very tame then you should consider releasing it in the spring in an area where it will not do harm, but not, of course, without the permission of the owner of the land.

Foxes can be very destructive animals, much as puppies are, and you should not consider taking on a fox cub if the family is going to mind about the odd pair of curtains being chewed or a hole dug in the carpet whilst the cub is young and needing to be with the family. It will be as well if the cub is accustomed from the start to spending the night in snug warm quarters of its own rather than in the house. Activities in the house should be supervised and as much time as possible should be spent inside with the family if you want it to be really tame. But when the cub is unsupervised at night is the time most of the damage will be done. Foxes are fascinating, and I greatly enjoyed the one which we had, though as my wife reminds me, I have conveniently forgotten some of the problems which we had to overcome. Foxes are very definitely only for experienced pet keepers with the right facilities and outlook. Unless you are prepared for the cub to be the centre of your family's life, do not be tempted!

There are various small mammals such as mice and voles which it is possible to catch and to keep and even breed in a tank set-up such as I have described above for other small mammals. They do not come into the category of simple pets, but for anyone who is a keen naturalist as well as an animal keeper, they can make a very interesting study.

There is one mammal, the hedgehog, which is attracted to our gardens because of the variety of food to be found there. Most of these hedgehogs are the descendants of those that lived on the farmland or waste ground before the houses were built and they have adapted readily to life in gardens. Because they are so easily attracted and are such beneficial animals to have in the garden it is possible to have a family of semi-tame hedgehogs living freely in the area. They will rapidly become accustomed to food and drink being put out for them, especially if this is done at a regular time. You should not give too much so that the hedgehog feeds only on your offering and ceases to hunt his territory for other things. Various things will attract hedgehogs, one of the best known being bread and milk. Hedgehogs are quite greedy animals and too much bread and milk is not good for them and can cause enteritis. They are meat and insect feeders so give only a little bread and milk together with meat. This can be tinned dog meat; some hedgehogs love this, others don't, some like one brand, others another. Hedgehogs are also voracious feeders on road casualty birds and rabbits so that any fresh carcasses will be eagerly devoured over several days. If you are going to feed your hedgehogs regularly it is a good idea to do so in a spot where you can watch them easily from the house and in a position where you can accustom them to a level of light that will enable you to look closely at them. This light should be introduced gradually and its intensity slowly increased once the hedgehogs are regular visitors.

Wild animals are most appreciated in their natural free state and I should like to think that keen pet lovers are also keen naturalists wanting to care for our own native wildlife as well for their pet. I have mentioned how you can help butterflies by encouraging them in your garden and it is also possible to encourage and help many of our wild birds as well. A lot of our birds are now very much dependent on us for their food and for places where they can build a nest and raise their young. We can help in several ways. Firstly, during the winter months especially, we can provide food and water for them. This is a time of year when many of our smaller birds would die if they did not feed each day. We can help by providing a range of foods such as waste bread, cereals, fruit, nuts, fat and seeds. Almost any waste household food will be eaten by one or more of the birds that visit our gardens. This can be scattered over the ground or placed higher up on a bird table carefully planned and sited so that birds have places where they can perch before approaching the table, and where cats cannot make an easy meal of the birds. Bags or small wire cages of peanuts hung up, the bones from the Sunday joint, and pieces of fat are attractive to the tit family and will ensure a regular stream of visitors. They become accustomed to human presence and many people hang the fat quite close to their window so that they can watch the birds at close hand. Sited by the kitchen window it can make even washing up seem fun! In addition to food birds also

Nest boxes suitable for robins (left) and tits (right)

need water and this should be provided as well both in winter (when it should be kept un-frozen) and summer. The birds will also continue to come for food much of the year although it is in winter when they need it most. Food supplies should be withdrawn in the late spring when natural food is available so that the young birds are fed a natural diet. The important thing with winter feeding is to make sure that it is done regularly each day, as otherwise birds that have learnt that you are a food source may well have difficulty in finding any other food if you do not feed them that day.

Many of the birds that have visited the garden for food can be encouraged to nest there. Shrubs, hedges and buildings will provide a number of possible sites and some planting with nesting birds in mind is a very good idea. Alternatively, or in addition, nest boxes can be provided at suitable points, but the size of the entrance hole will need to be adjusted otherwise they will fill up almost at once with sparrows and starlings and the smaller birds such as the tits and robins won't get a look in. Properly done your garden could become a very interesting and attractive nature reserve in its own right.

Books about pets

Here is a short list of books which you will find useful and interesting to read. Publishers' names are given in brackets. Some may no longer be in print, but you should be able to borrow most of them from your local library.

General
Caring for your Pet by Howard Loxton (David & Charles)
Pets for Children by Stephanie and Ken Denham (Hamlyn)
Phil Drabble's Book of Pets by Phil Drabble (Fontana)

Dogs
Dog Care by Wendy Boorer (Hamlyn)
Dogs by Wendy Boorer (Hamlyn)

Cats
Cats by Christine Metcalf (Hamlyn)

Mice and Rats
Mice and Rats by K. W. Smith (Bartholomew)

Hamsters and Gerbils
Hamsters and Gerbils by K. W. Smith (Bartholomew)

Birds
Beginner's Guide to Birdkeeping by Rosemary Low (Pelham)
Pet Birds by Cyril Rogers (Hamlyn)
The Book of Cage Birds by Charles Trevisick

Horses and Ponies
Buying and Keeping a Horse or Pony, Caring for a Horse or Pony by Robert Owen and John Bullock (Beaver)

Aquarium species
The Clue Book of Freshwater Animals by Gwen Allen and Joan Denslow (Oxford University Press)
The Coral Coldwater Fish Book (Liverine)
Tortoises and Terrapins (Colourmaster)
Tropical Freshwater Aquaria by George Cust and Peter Bird (Hamlyn)
Your Aquarium (Colourmaster)

Pond Life
Pond Life in the Aquarium by Horst Janus (Studio Vista)
Your Garden Pond (Colourmaster)

Index

# More Beaver Books

We hope you have enjoyed this Beaver Book. Here are some of the other titles:

Looking at Wildlife A Beaver original. Nicholas Hammond has written an invaluable guide for young naturalists, with lots of information on all kinds of wild creatures as well as advice on the best ways of observing them. Illustrated throughout

Exploring Nature A Beaver original. Make earthworms come at your command, learn the secret of the oak gall and discover how a fairy ring grows – just a few of the many exciting projects in this book for the budding naturalist. Written by Derek Hall and illustrated by Tony Morris

The Mine Kid Kidnap A week's holiday in Wales for a party of London schoolchildren turns into a thrilling adventure, but when a girl is kidnapped the adventure becomes a real matter of life and death. An exciting and amusing story for readers of nine upwards by Eve Jennings

Beaver Crossword Book 3 A Beaver original. Eighty more crosswords for you to solve, graded from fairly easy to really tricky! Compiled by Pat Duncan.

These and many other Beavers are available at your local bookshop or newsagent, or can be ordered direct from: Hamlyn Paperback Cash Sales, PO Box 11, Falmouth, Cornwall TR10 9EN. Send a cheque or postal order, made payable to The Hamlyn Publishing Group, for the price of the book plus postage at the following rates:
UK: 22p for the first book plus 10p a copy for each extra book ordered to a maximum of 92p;
BFPO and EIRE: 22p for the first book plus 10p a copy for the next 6 books and thereafter 4p a book;
OVERSEAS: 30p for the first book and 10p for each extra book

New Beavers are published every month and if you would like the *Beaver Bulletin*, which gives a complete list of books and prices, including new titles send a large stamped addressed envelope to:

Beaver Bulletin,
The Hamlyn Group
Astronaut House
Feltham
Middlesex TW14 9AR